EVENTS THAT
CHANGED THE
WORLD

1980–2000

— The Twentieth Century —

1980–2000

══ The Twentieth Century ══

Other books in the
Events That Changed the World series:

1980–2000

═ The Twentieth Century ═

Bryan Grapes, *Book Editor*

Daniel Leone, *President*
Bonnie Szumski, *Publisher*
Scott Barbour, *Managing Editor*

**GREENHAVEN
PRESS®**

THOMSON
─────※─────™
GALE

San Diego • Detroit • New York • San Francisco • Cleveland
New Haven, Conn. • Waterville, Maine • London • Munich

THOMSON

─────✦───── ™

GALE

LIBRARY OF CONGRESS CATALOGING-IN-PUBLICATION DATA

1980–2000 / Bryan Grapes, book editor.
    p. cm. — (Events that changed the world)
    Includes bibliographical references and index.
    ISBN 0-7377-1760-2 (lib. bdg. : alk. paper) —
    ISBN 0-7377-1761-0 (pbk. : alk. paper)
    1. World politics—1975–1985—Sources. 2. World politics—1985–1995—Sources. I. Grapes, Bryan. II. Series.
    D856.A17 2004
    909.82'8—dc21   2003053928

Printed in the United States of America

CONTENTS

Event 1: The AIDS Epidemic Begins: June 5, 1981

1. The AIDS Epidemic Has a Long-Range Impact

by Sabin Russell   24

Since its discovery in the early 1980s, AIDS has claimed more than 20 million lives and sparked significant changes in society's approach toward sexual politics, health care, drug use, and sex education.

2. Doctors Encounter the First Wave of AIDS Patients

by Ronald Bayer and Gerald M. Oppenheimer   31

The doctors who treated the first wave of AIDS patients in the 1980s were forced to confront not only a new medical ailment but also a social world that few of them had encountered.

Event 2: MTV Begins Broadcasting: August 1, 1981

1. MTV Changes the Music World

by Carla Hay   45

Though music videos had existed before MTV debuted in 1981, few in the music world took them seriously. In less than a decade, few could name a music superstar who did not have a video in regular rotation on MTV.

Event 6: The Chinese Government Crushes Student Demonstrations in Tiananmen Square: June 4, 1989

Event 7: The Berlin Wall Falls: November 9, 1989

Event 8: The First World Wide Web Is Launched: December 12, 1991

1. The Creation of the Web

In 1991, after developing a language called hypertext transfer protocol, physicist Tim Berners-Lee and his colleague Robert Calliau went online with the world's first World Wide Web server and forever changed the way people access information and conduct business.

Event 9: The Soviet Union Dissolves: December 25, 1991

1. The Death of the Soviet Union Shatters the Old World Order

The death of the Soviet Union has had profound geopolitical consequences. The Soviet Union's collapse has made the world a more diverse and unpredictable place.

2. Mikhail Gorbachev's Resignation Speech

Soviet president Mikhail Gorbachev recalls the reforms he initiated during his reign, outlines his reasons for stepping down, and voices his reservations and hopes for the future of the former Soviet republics.

Event 10: South Africa Holds Its First Multiracial Elections: April 29, 1994

1. The Election Marks the Birth of Genuine Democracy in South Africa

Four years after its Parliament repealed apartheid, South Africa held the first multiracial election in its history. The African National Congress won the majority of seats in the new government, and Nel-

son Mandela was sworn in as the nation's first
black president.

Event 11: Israeli Prime Minister Yitzhak Rabin Is Assassinated: November 4, 1995

1. Rabin's Assassination Ruins a Landmark Chance for Peace

by Michael Karpin and Ina Friedman
After signing the Oslo Accords with Palestinian
leader Yasser Arafat, Israeli prime minister
Yitzhak Rabin was vilified as a traitor by the conservative elements of his government and the
press. This charged atmosphere of hate may have
led to his death at the hands of a right-wing zealot.

Event 12: Dolly the Sheep Is Cloned: July 5, 1996

1. The Medical and Scientific Significance of Dolly's Birth

by Marie A. DiBerardino
The birth of the first mammal cloned from an adult
cell will profoundly affect the way doctors treat
such maladies as hemophilia, cystic fibrosis, and
heart disease. It will also lessen complications associated with organ transplants and help in the fight
against birth defects.

2. Ian Wilmut Addresses the Questions Raised by Dolly's Birth

by Andrew Ross
Wilmut argues that despite the potential for misuse, cloning has incredible potential for good in
the medical field and explains his stance against
human cloning.

I n 1543 a Polish astronomer named Nicolaus Copernicus published a book entitled *De revolutionibus orbium coelestium* in which he theorized that Earth revolved around the Sun. In 1688, during the Glorious Revolution, Dutch prince William of Orange invaded England and overthrew King James II. In 1922 Irish author James Joyce's novel *Ulysses*, which describes one day in Dublin, was published.

Although these events are seemingly unrelated, occurring in different nations and in different centuries, they all share the distinction of having changed the world. Although Copernicus's book had a relatively minor impact at the time of its publication, it eventually had a momentous influence. The Copernican system provided a foundation on which future scientists could develop an accurate understanding of the solar system. Perhaps more importantly, it required humanity to contemplate the possibility that Earth, far from occupying a special place at the center of creation, was merely one planet in a vast universe. In doing so, it forced a reevaluation of the Christian cosmology that had served as the foundation of Western culture. As professor Thomas S. Kuhn writes, "The drama of Christian life and the morality that had been made dependent upon it would not readily adapt to a universe in which the earth was just one of a number of planets."

Like the Copernican revolution, the Glorious Revolution of 1688–1689 had a profound influence on the future of Western societies. By deposing James II, William and his wife, Mary, ended the Stuart dynasty, a series of monarchs who had favored the Catholic Church and had limited the power of Parliament for decades. Under William and Mary, Parliament passed the Bill of Rights, which established the legislative supremacy of Parliament and barred Roman Catholics from the throne. These actions initiated the gradual process by which the power of the government of England shifted from the monarchy to Parliament, establishing a democratic system that would be copied, with some variations, by the United States and other democratic societies worldwide.

Whereas the Glorious Revolution had a major impact in the political sphere, the publication of Joyce's novel *Ulysses* represented a revolution in literature. In an effort to capture the sense of chaos and discontinuity that permeated the culture in the wake of World War I, Joyce did away with the use of straightforward narrative that had dominated fiction up to that time. The novel, whose structure mirrors that of Homer's *Odyssey*, combines realistic descriptions of events with passages that convey the characters' inner experience by means of a technique known as stream of consciousness, in which the characters' thoughts and feelings are presented without regard to logic or narrative order. Due to its departure from the traditional modes of fiction, *Ulysses* is often described as one of the seminal works of modernist literature. As stated by Pennsylvania State University professor Michael H. Begnal, "*Ulysses* is the novel that changed the direction of 20th-century fiction written in English."

Copernicus's theory of a sun-centered solar system, the Glorious Revolution, and James Joyce's *Ulysses* are just three examples of time-bound events that have had far-reaching effects—for better or worse—on the progress of human societies worldwide. History is made up of an inexhaustible list of such events. In the twentieth century alone, for example, one can isolate any number of world-shattering moments: the first performance of Igor Stravinsky's ballet *The Rites of Spring* in 1913; Japan's attack on Pearl Harbor on December 7, 1941; the launch of the satellite *Sputnik* on October 4, 1957. These events variously influenced the culture, society, and political configuration of the twentieth century.

Greenhaven Press's Events That Changed the World series is designed to help readers learn about world history by examining seemingly random events that have had the greatest influence on the development of cultures, societies, and governments throughout the ages. The series is divided into sets of several anthologies, with each set covering a period of one hundred years. Each volume begins with an introduction that provides essential context on the time period being covered. Then, the major events of the era are covered by means of primary and secondary sources. Primary sources include firsthand accounts, speeches, correspondence, and other materials that bring history alive. Secondary sources analyze the profound effects the events had on the world. Each reading is preceded by an introduction that puts it in context and emphasizes the event's importance in the ongoing evolution of world history. Additional features add to the value of the series: An annotated table of contents and an index allow readers to quickly locate material of interest. A chronology provides an easy reference for contextual information. And a bibliography offers opportunities for further exploration. All of these features help to make the Events That Changed the World series a valuable resource for readers interested in the major events that have shaped the course of humanity.

Toward a New World Order

On Christmas Day 1991, Mikhail Gorbachev resigned as president of the Soviet Union, officially declaring the seventy year-old Communist state defunct. Gorbachev's announcement was anticlimactic; a series of events throughout the year had made it clear that the union's days were numbered. Indeed, two weeks earlier, leaders of several member states—including Russia—had declared the end of the Soviet Union. Nevertheless, although it was a formality, Gorbachev's resignation was the symbolic final act of a once-formidable nation.

The end of the Soviet Union, coming with a quiet Christmas Day statement, was not necessarily the most dramatic event of the period 1980 to 2000. Other events of the era certainly created more compelling news stories. The space shuttle *Challenger* explosion in 1986, the Chernobyl nuclear disaster in Ukraine that same year, the 1989 crackdown against prodemocracy protesters in Tiananmen Square in China, civil war in the former Yugoslavia, and genocide in the African nation of Rwanda in the early 1990s—all of these events were dramatic, shocking, and often horrifying. However, despite its relative lack of dramatics, the collapse of the Soviet Union had profound consequences for the world. Not only did it mark the end of a country, it brought an end to a global balance of power between the United States and the Soviet state that had dominated global affairs for over forty years. As a result, the United States was left as the world's only remaining superpower struggling to redefine itself in a world with no major enemy but many regional crises and conflicts.

The Roots of an Empire's Decline

At its apex, the Soviet Union was a sprawling nation that consisted of fifteen republics in north Asia and east Europe, with Russia at its center. In addition to these republics, numerous other nations—often referred to as satellite states—fell under the Soviet sway. These countries were not part of the union per se but received financial support in return for their loyalty, trade, and ideological adherence to the Communist system. The most strategically important of these states were those of Eastern Europe, including East Germany, Czechoslovakia, Hungary, and Poland, but others could be found in Africa, Asia, and Latin America.

When discussing the collapse of the Soviet Union, experts often distinguish between internal and external causes. One of the major internal causes was economic. Many commentators stress the inefficiency of the Soviet economic system. Although ostensibly based on a Communist model, most aspects of the economy and industry were controlled by the state. This central control resulted in the creation of a massive bureaucracy that was often inefficient and corrupt. Under this system, agriculture and industry both suffered. By the mid-1980s the Soviet Union and most of its satellites lagged behind the Western democracies (as well as Communist China) economically. At the same time that its agriculture and industry were flailing, the nation spent huge sums of money to prop up Communist regimes around the world. In 1979 Soviet leaders made what proved to be a fateful decision when they sent troops to Afghanistan to support an embattled Communist leader there. Various Afghan tribal factions that ordinarily opposed one another joined forces to fight the Soviets. As a result, the Soviet army got bogged down in a costly losing battle, ultimately withdrawing in defeat in 1989.

Perhaps the most significant internal causes of the collapse of the Soviet Union were the policies of Gorbachev himself. When Gorbachev came to power in 1985, he inherited economic and political systems that were in crisis. He quickly instituted a series of social, economic, and political reforms designed to save the ailing system. Under glasnost (openness), restrictions on speech were relaxed and an honest examination of the misdeeds of former Soviet leaders (especially Lenin) was encouraged. Perestroika (restructuring) was an attempt to repair the economy by reducing the system's bureaucracy. *Demokratizatsiya* (democratization) was an attempt to inject elements of democracy into the Soviet political system. Taken together, these and other reforms amounted to an overall relaxing of a system that had theretofore been tightly controlled, including periodic violent crackdowns on protests and harsh punishment of dissidents.

Rather than serving to modernize the socialist system, loosening up its ideology and structure simply undermined it and, some say, led to its ultimate demise. Glasnost and democratization allowed citizens to express their dissatisfaction with the Soviet system and to begin alternative political movements. Meanwhile, economic reforms failed to save the ailing economy. Writing soon after the Soviet Union's demise, Michael Mandelbaum, a professor at the Paul H. Nitze School of Advanced International Studies, cogently summed up Gorbachev's contribution to his nation's unraveling:

> His aim had been to strengthen the political and economic systems that he inherited . . . and make the Soviet Union a modern dynamic state. Instead he had fatally weakened it. Intending to reform Soviet communism he had, rather, destroyed it. The three major policies that he had launched to fashion a more efficient and humane form of socialism—glasnost, democratization and perestroika— had in the end subverted, discredited and all but done away with the network of political and economic institutions his Communist Party had constructed in Russia and surrounding countries since 1917.[1]

Aside from these internal forces, some claim that external forces helped to bring about the end of the Soviet Union and the Cold War. Specifically, these historians credit the U.S. policy of confrontation adopted by President Ronald Reagan during his tenure from 1980 to 1988. For decades both sides had engaged in an arms race, with each side attempting to outpace the other on the number and destructive capacity of their nuclear arsenals. Eventually it had become evident that both sides had enough nuclear weapons to completely destroy the enemy even if the enemy struck first. Thus equilibrium had been reached, a situation referred to as mutually assured destruction (MAD); in case of war, regardless of who struck first, both sides would be annihilated. It was hoped that this threat of guaranteed destruction would keep both sides from launching an attack.

Reagan seemed to break this deadlock with his Strategic Defense Initiative (SDI). This project, which was dubbed "Star

Wars" by its critics, was an ambitious plan to develop a system of space-based missiles that could defend the nation in case of a Soviet first strike. This system threatened to shift the balance in favor of the United States by allowing America to fend off all attacks. Some historians contend that Gorbachev knew that he could not afford a similar system, and that therefore he had no alternative but to negotiate on arms with the United States, essentially conceding defeat.

The Empire Succumbs

As a result of the changes wrought under Gorbachev, by 1989 it was clear that the Cold War was coming to an end. That year, popular uprisings in several of the union's European satellite states led to the overthrow of Communist leaders in favor of more democratic systems of government. The most dramatic, although by no means the most violent, of these revolutions took place in East Germany. On November 9, after weeks of protests and mass defections, the Berlin Wall—the most powerful symbol of the Cold War—was breached as authorities passively looked on. All night long, citizens held a party on and around the wall—actions for which they would have been shot in previous years. Robert Darnton, a professor of European history at Princeton University, vividly described the events of November 9 in his book *Berlin Journal, 1989–1990:*

> One [East Berliner], a young man with a knapsack on his back, somehow hoisted himself up on the Wall directly across from the Brandenburg Gate. He sauntered along the top of it . . ., a perfect target for the bullets that had felled many other wall jumpers. . . .
>
> A few minutes later, hundreds of people . . . were on the Wall, embracing, dancing, exchanging flowers, drinking wine, helping up new "conquerors"—and chipping away at the Wall itself. By midnight, under a full moon and the glare of spotlights in no man's land, a thousand figures swarmed over the Wall, hammering, chiseling, wearing its surface away like a colony of army ants.[2]

By the end of 1989, Czechoslovakia and Hungary had joined East Germany in beginning the process of dismantling their Communist governments. Romania, which had a Communist government that was independent of the Soviet Union, experienced a violent revolution as well.

By turning away from communism, the European satellite states ended their alliance with their former sponsors in the Soviet Union, thus weakening the union's economy and military might and diminishing the threat of communism. In 1990 the union was further weakened by events within its own borders. Having witnessed the revolutions of Europe, nationalists within various Soviet republics began to demonstrate for independence. As J.M. Roberts, warden at Melton College at Oxford University, notes, Gorbachev's reforms helped to create the conditions for these protests by allowing underlying nationalist and regional allegiances to surface and find expression:

> The thawing of the iron grip of the past had revealed the power of nationalist and regional sentiment when excited by economic collapse and opportunity. After seventy years of efforts to make Soviet citizens, the USSR was revealed to be a collection of peoples as distinct as ever, organized in fifteen republics, some of which (above all the three Baltic republics of Latvia, Estonia and Lithuania) were quick to show dissatisfaction with their lot and, in the end, were to lead the way to political change.[3]

The three Baltic states declared their independence in 1990, and Gorbachev struggled to keep the union together by means of concessions and power-sharing arrangements.

The final blow to the Soviet Union came in the summer of 1991. On August 19, the day before Gorbachev was scheduled to sign a new Union Treaty that would have given greater power to the republics, nine hard-line members of the Communist Party attempted to wrest control of the country. Although the coup plotters arrested Gorbachev, they failed to arrest Boris Yeltsin, the popularly elected president of the Russian Republic, who rallied an opposition to the takeover. In the end, failing to gain popular, international, or military support, the coup failed, and Gorbachev was returned to power. However, the bungled coup had exposed the obsolescence of communism in the Soviet Union. Gorbachev, failing to acknowledge this new reality, persisted in his attempts to keep the union together. Despite his efforts, by December 21, fourteen of the fifteen republics had declared the end of the Soviet Union (only the republic of Georgia, engaged in a civil war of its own, did not make a formal announcement). By the end of the year, the fifteen republics were independent nations.

A New World Order

The end of the Cold War and the disintegration of the Soviet Union truly changed the world. For the previous four decades, since the end of World War II, global politics had been dominated by two superpowers. All of the world's major conflicts, trading partnerships, and security alliances had been predicated on this bipolar orientation. Now, in a few short years, the foundation of the international order had been undermined. Where there were formally two superpowers, there was now only one: the United States of America.

Many commentators expressed optimism that this state of affairs would result in a "new world order" in which the international community—led by the United Nations and with U.S. assistance—would cooperate to resolve conflicts, maintain peace, and provide humanitarian assistance when necessary. Indeed, the 1990s began with a positive example of this idea in action. In 1991, in response to Iraq's invasion of its neighbor Kuwait, the United States led a broad coalition of forces, sanctioned by the United Nations, to repel Iraqi troops and restore the integrity of Kuwait. U.S. president George H.W. Bush, in describing his rationale for the war, articulated his conception of the new world order:

> This is an historic moment. We have in this past year [1990] made great progress in ending the long era of conflict and cold war. We have before us the opportunity to forge for ourselves and for future generations a new world order—a world where the rule of law, not the rule of the jungle, governs the conduct of nations. . . . We have a real chance at this new world order, an order in which a credible United Nations can use its peacekeeping role to fulfill the promise and vision of the U.N.'s founders.[4]

Despite Bush's optimistic vision of international cooperation, it quickly became apparent that the post–Cold War world would not be without its own problems. Indeed, although Soviet-style communism had kept millions of people living under various degrees of oppression, the ideological battle between the Communist East and capitalist West had imposed a measure of stability on the world. As the British journal the *Economist* put it in 1992:

> The cold war had one claim to merit: it was a system of discipline. Most countries, in most parts of the world, belonged in some degree to one or the other of a pair of teams. If a member of one team

got into an argument with a member of the other team, he could appeal to his team leader for help. Since the team leaders did not wish to fight each other, they would generally urge restraint. . . .

This was a powerful preserver of stability: not only stability between countries, but stability inside them as well.[5]

With the end of the Cold War, this "preserver of stability" was removed. Consequently, according to the *Economist*, "The collapse of communism has not had the effect, as many people thought it would, of reducing the number of smaller, less-than-global causes of trouble. On the contrary, it is producing more of them."[6] Indeed, according to the National Defense Council Foundation, by 2000 the number of nations experiencing violent conflict had nearly doubled since the height of the Cold War.

The country that perhaps best illustrates the post–Cold War dilemma is Yugoslavia. Created at the end of World War I, Yugoslavia consisted of six republics, most notably Serbia, Croatia, and Bosnia. These republics were occupied by various ethnic groups—including Serbs, Croats, and Muslims—that bore intense, long-standing hostilities toward one another. Complicating this situation was the fact that these ethnic groups were not isolated within their own republics but were instead scattered throughout the nation, many in enclaves within republics dominated by their enemies. The Communist dictator Marshal Tito had kept these hostilities suppressed until his death in 1980. Subsequent leaders had also managed to maintain order until the early 1990s. In June 1991, the republics of Croatia and Slovenia declared their independence from Yugoslavia. The Serbs acted militarily to prevent this secession, thus initiating a civil war that would erupt sporadically in various republics throughout the decade.

The most intense fighting began in 1992, when Bosnia declared its independence. The Serbs within Bosnia opposed secession and declared war on the Yugoslav government. The resulting war lasted until 1995 and killed two hundred thousand people, created 2 million refugees, and left widespread destruction of the region's infrastructure. Perhaps the most disturbing aspects of the war were the techniques the Serbs, led by Slobodan Milosovic, used against their enemies, especially the Croats and Muslims. In a practice known as "ethnic cleansing," they forced civilians from their homes and villages, often leaving destroyed villages in their wake. They also conducted mass executions and housed civilians in concentration camps reminiscent of those used in Nazi Germany.

The war in Bosnia seemed to dispel any hopes for a new world order. With no superpower rivalry to impose order, ancient hostilities came to the surface and spilled over in a paroxysm of violence. Meanwhile, the international community mostly watched and did nothing. Why did the world fail to act? As the world's only superpower, the United States would have been the likely candidate to lead an intervention. However, America, like other Western nations, had little economic or political interest in the region. The majority of Americans were not willing to risk the lives of U.S. soldiers under these circumstances. Moreover, although the Cold War was over, Russia, the largest of the former Soviet republics and a major power in its own right, had a historical affinity with the Serbs. U.S. leaders feared that any significant move against the Serbs could antagonize Russia at a time of sensitive U.S.-Russia relations. For these reasons, the United States made only limited symbolic and diplomatic efforts to address the crisis. Other Western powers were equally reluctant to get involved. The North Atlantic Treaty Organization (NATO), an alliance of nations dedicated to the security of Western Europe and North America, was unwilling to commit significant resources due to a lack of international support.

In 1999 the new world order was again put to the test in Bosnia when Kosovo, a republic of Bosnia inhabited mostly by ethnic Albanians, sought independence. The Kosovo Liberation Army (KLA) began attacking Serbian troops and police. The Serbs, led by Slobodan Milosevic, attempted to prevent Kosovo's secession by force, resorting to tactics similar to those they used in the early 1990s. When negotiations failed to end the conflict, NATO, with major U.S. assistance, began a bombing campaign against the Bosnian Serbs that would last eleven weeks. Although NATO eventually prevailed, succeeding in driving the Bosnian Serbs from Kosovo, the intervention was controversial. Some argued that the bombing merely provoked Milosevic and the Serbs to new heights of violence before ultimately withdrawing. In the end, more than eight hundred thousand Kosovar civilians were forced from the country and ten thousand were killed. Moreover, while some heralded the NATO action as a precedent—the beginning of a new era of humanitarian intervention—it turned out to be an isolated incident. Despite this one notable exception of international cooperation, as the twentieth century ended the United States continued its noninterventionist foreign policy approach.

Unfortunately, Bosnia was not the only area of the world to experience major conflict and upheaval in the post–Cold War era. As if to confirm the death of the new world order, similar scenarios played out in various African and Asian nations throughout the 1990s. In response, the United States chose to intervene rarely and minimally, if at all. The most disturbing example of America's hands-off foreign policy occurred in 1994, when genocide in Rwanda left over five hundred thousand people dead in the space of one hundred days while the international community watched and the UN actually decreased its presence in the nation.

The events of September 11, 2001, would eventually result in a drastic change in U.S. foreign policy by initiating an era of unilateral military intervention, including another war in Iraq. But in the 1990s, in the period between the Cold War and the war on terrorism, Americans were content to focus on domestic concerns rather than regional conflicts in far-flung corners of the world.

Notes

1. Michael Mandelbaum, "Coup de Grace: The End of the Soviet Union," *Foreign Affairs*, Autumn/Winter 1991–1992.

2. Robert Darnton, *Berlin Journal, 1989–1990*. New York: W.W. Norton, 1991.

3. J.M. Roberts, *History of the World*. New York: Oxford University Press, 1993, p. 907.

4. George H.W. Bush, televised address to the American people, January 16, 1991.

5. *Economist*, "Meet Your Unbrave New World," September 5, 1992.

6. *Economist*, "Meet Your Unbrave New World."

The AIDS Epidemic Has a Long-Range Impact

by Sabin Russell

In the late 1970s doctors on both coasts of the United States had started to encounter an increasing caseload of inexplicable and untreatable immunological maladies in previously healthy men, women, and children. By 1981 health care professionals in New York and California were regularly recording cases of very rare disorders, such as Kaposi's sarcoma and cytomegalovirus, as well as Pneumocystis carinii pneumonia (PCP). These diseases were usually seen only in severely immune-suppressed people, and doctors were at a loss to explain the sudden frequency with which they were encountering new cases. In late 1980 and early 1981, Michael Gottlieb, an immunologist at the University of California at Los Angeles, suspected that a new ailment was afoot. He began to put together a study that documented the cases of five previously healthy homosexual men in the Los Angeles area who had all developed PCP. This landmark study, which appeared in *Morbidity and Mortality Weekly Report* on June 5, 1981, marked the official beginning of the AIDS crisis. In the following essay Sabin Russell, medical writer for the *San Francisco Chronicle*, charts the worldwide course of the disease and its impact on society.

In 2001 the global death toll from AIDS reached 20 million. Russell points out that although the disease was once thought of as a problem concerning only the urban gay communities of the United States, AIDS was soon recognized as a global problem that cut across racial, social, gender, and sexual lines. The disease has taken a particularly dreadful turn in Africa and Asia, where poverty, war, poor sanitation, lack of proper medical facilities, and access to drugs has fueled a devastating rise in the caseload, Russell argues.

Russell points out that AIDS has also had profound social implications. In efforts to prevent the spread of the disease, frank discussions about sexuality, gay marriage, drug use, condoms, and sexually transmitted diseases were pushed to the forefront of public debate. The rise of AIDS also forced the public to confront discrimination against homosexuals. Political strategies adopted by AIDS activists to pressure the government to commit money to the fight against the disease has inspired other groups, Russell states, most notably those who are fighting the war against breast and prostate cancer. Unfortunately, Russell points out, despite the billions of dollars committed to preventing and curing AIDS, the disease is still cutting a swath of misery throughout the world.

[O n June 5, 2001,] the world marks 20 years of AIDS. It is a ghastly anniversary, especially for San Francisco, where the epidemic touched down early and devastated a generation of gay men.

Like a disaster in slow motion, AIDS has taken 18,600 San Francisco lives, far more than the city lost in wars and earthquakes and fires combined.

"It hurts me the most when I remember the good times," said AIDS activist Cleve Jones, 46, a long-term survivor who has beaten the odds. "I would love to reach out and pick up the phone and say, 'Hey, do you remember when we did that?' There is hardly anyone left in my life who knew me when I was young."

Two decades ago, nobody ever thought it would last this long. No one could have imagined how terrible it would become.

But since June 5, 1981, when doctors described an outbreak of rare pneumonia among five gay men in Los Angeles, AIDS has rewritten the rule book.

It is changing how neighborhoods and nations alike respond to disease. It is changing how medical research is conducted, how drugs are approved and sold. It is changing both sexual behavior and attitudes toward sexuality. It is changing how we live, and even how we die.

Once thought of as a "gay disease" afflicting only the hip, urban centers of America, AIDS is now unmasked as a global killer whose toll has passed the 20 million dead of the Spanish influenza of 1918. It has cut a swath through impoverished African states and is now threatening the teeming populations of India, China and Southeast Asia.

A medical curiosity in 1981, AIDS was declared a threat to national security [in 2000]. This month, it will be the focus of an unprecedented special session of the U.N. General Assembly.

"From the start, HIV has always been a political disease," said Paul Volberding, who saw his first case of AIDS on his first day on the job at San Francisco General Hospital, 20 years ago.

Belated Global Mobilization Now Afoot

Just as AIDS activism transformed the politics of medicine in America, HIV is stirring the revolutionary embers of post-apartheid South Africa and a belated global mobilization is now afoot.

The marches in Johannesburg, the vocal protests against unresponsive governments and wealthy drug companies, and the demands for dollars for research and treatment for Africa are an echo of the ferment that began in San Francisco two decades ago.

In the early years of the epidemic, no place was hit harder than the gay community here, where up to half the men were infected with HIV. With its tolerance, free spirit and love of the outlandish, San Francisco was a sexual carnival that created laboratory-like conditions for breeding a new virus.

AIDS arrived during a time of political upheaval. The city was at the forefront of the movement for gay civil rights, and was still reeling from the 1978 assassinations of gay Supervisor Harvey Milk and Mayor George Moscone.

Landing atop this political tinderbox, AIDS unleashed a swarm of activism, community compassion and civic generosity that still has widespread effects today.

Even as the gay community warred with itself—over issues such as closure of public sex bathhouses—a new code of safe sex took hold and dramatically reduced transmission rates of the virus.

Then, activists confronted drug companies and the Food and Drug Administration, demanding access to experimental treatments, humanely designed drug trials and speedy approval of

People view the AIDS memorial quilt in Washington, D.C.
More than 20 million people worldwide have died from
AIDS.

new medications. The changes have stuck.

"I don't think you can do research anymore without advocates
involved in the design of clinical trials," said Donald Abrams, an
AIDS specialist at San Francisco General Hospital.

The striking success of AIDS activism—an arsenal of new
drugs that cut the death rate in half, and a federal war chest that
commits U.S. $7.5 billion a year for research, prevention, treat-
ment and care—is being emulated around the globe.

Women with breast cancer were first to take up the tactics of
AIDS activists. Men with prostate cancer followed suit. Anti-
smoking activists have taken on the tobacco industry, and advocates for the mentally ill have forcefully brought their case for
parity to the public.

"AIDS activism is getting diseases out of the shadows and into the light," said Sally Coates, director of the San Francisco office of the Susan G. Komen Foundation, which raises funds to fight breast cancer.

The AIDS Emergency Fund, established in 1982 to help sick patients meet the rent or pay utility bills, has just initiated the Breast Cancer Emergency Fund, which provides similar grants to women battling that disease.

"The people at AIDS Emergency Fund said they wanted to give something back to the women who gave so much to them during the AIDS epidemic," said Coates.

The Courage of Those Afflicted Earned the Respect of Millions of Americans

As the epidemic ravaged San Francisco's gay community it paradoxically strengthened it, and the courage of those afflicted earned the respect of millions of Americans who were either indifferent or hostile to the civil rights issues of homosexuals.

Struggles for health insurance coverage and survival benefits have underscored the inequity of the ban on gay marriage, and sparked a national movement for civil unions.

The lesbian community in San Francisco—once almost as insulated from gay male culture as straights—rushed to the aid of the stricken, forming personal and political ties that endure.

The AIDS years are etched into memories, not only of those who survive with the disease, but also of those who cared for the sick and dying, and those who were friends and neighbors of those who died.

Sandra Hernandez, San Francisco's former public health director, arrived at San Francisco General Hospital in 1984 as a young medical resident. "It was like wartime," she recalled. "On any given night, you might pronounce three or four patients dead."

In her last year of residency, her brother died of AIDS in Arizona. He was 31.

"You can describe it as catastrophic, on one hand," said Hernandez. "On the other hand, there are profound lessons to be learned from people who are facing mortality about what is important in life and what is not."

David Rousseau, a 36-year-old gay man, died of AIDS on June 19, 1991, but his straight friend Charlene Smith still treasures her time with him.

She cared for him as he lay dying of Kaposi's sarcoma, applying a sticky ointment to his lesions. "His legs were blistered, like they had been burned," she said. "It took almost two hours to change the bandages on his legs and feet."

After Rousseau died, Smith signed up as a hospice volunteer and spent two more years comforting strangers fighting their last battle with AIDS.

"I thought to myself that David wouldn't die because I loved him so much," Smith said. "I know that doesn't make sense, but I also know I'm not the only one who ever felt that way."

AIDS in San Francisco has been "a time of unspeakable horror, and a time of great grace," said Jim Mitulski, 43, former pastor of the Metropolitan Community Church in the heart of the Castro district. During the worst period, he conducted more than 500 funerals, most of them of gay men his own age.

Gay weddings took on a new significance, as well. "When we say, 'in sickness and in health, till death do us part,' it really means something to us," Mitulski said.

Like the scattered ashes of the dead, there is today little overt evidence of catastrophe in San Francisco. Daily life in the Castro district goes on—even as it managed to do at the height of the death and dying.

AIDS Prevention Efforts Changed the Urban Landscape

Yet AIDS prevention efforts have literally changed the urban landscape. In San Francisco, buses prowl the neighborhoods bearing ads with explicit and erotic imagery urging men to question their assumptions about the HIV status of their partners.

AIDS has forced a frank and open discussion of sexuality, gay and straight, into the early years of education. These days, kindergartners are cautioned that germs are found in blood, fifth-graders are told about oral and anal sex, and high schoolers are offered lessons on how to wear a condom.

"This is a generation that has never not known HIV, just as their parents had never not known The Bomb," said Trish Bascom, San Francisco's director of school health programs.

Twenty years of AIDS has driven issues such as assisted suicide, needle exchange and the medical use of marijuana into the mainstream of American politics—winning grassroots support and initiative campaigns, but condemnation from the federal government.

Yet with all these dramatic shifts, some still question whether things have changed enough.

Marcus Conant, a University of California at San Francisco dermatologist who was engaged in the battle from the earliest days, has seen a holocaust up close and fears for the future.

New drugs have hobbled the virus, but may have also weakened prevention efforts. Even in San Francisco, a city that has lost so many, the ethic of safe sex is slipping, and sexually transmitted diseases are increasing. "What's to say that the virus won't win?" said Conant. "Maybe this is the thing that's going to wipe us all out."

Two decades after its presence was first detected, AIDS remains very much among us. It continues to kill. It continues to build a legacy of social transformation. Unfortunately for us all, AIDS at 20 is still a work in progress.

Doctors Encounter the First Wave of AIDS Patients

by Ronald Bayer and Gerald M. Oppenheimer

In the following piece Ronald Bayer and Gerald M. Oppenheimer chronicle the recollections of Michael Gottlieb and other doctors who treated the first wave of AIDS patients in the early 1980s. The health care professionals interviewed by Bayer and Oppenheimer recall how the disease pushed them into uncharted waters, not only in medical terms but in social terms as well. AIDS also forced a frank discussion of sexuality, sexual habits, and drug use. For the first time, many of these doctors found themselves taking sexual histories of the patients they were treating. In doing so, many were exposed to a world they never knew existed. When it was discovered that sexual lifestyle strongly correlated with the spread of the disease, many of these physicians found themselves in the position of having to dictate changes in sexual habits. Ronald Bayer is a professor of public health at the Joseph L. Mailman School of Public Health at Columbia University. Gerald M. Oppenheimer is a professor of public health at Brooklyn College and an associate professor of clinical public health at the Joseph L. Mailman School of Public Health. They are coauthors of *AIDS Doctors: Voices from the Epidemic: An Oral History*, from which this essay is excerpted.

In the period October 1980–May 1981, 5 young men, all active homosexuals, were treated for biopsy-confirmed *Pneumocystis*

Ronald Bayer and Gerald M. Oppenheimer, *AIDS Doctors: Voices from the Epidemic: An Oral History*. New York: Oxford University Press, 2000. Copyright © 2000 by Ronald Bayer and Gerald M. Oppenheimer. Reproduced by permission of the publisher.

carinii pneumonia at 3 different hospitals in Los Angeles, California. Two of the patients died. . . . *Pneumocystis* pneumonia in the United States is almost exclusively limited to severely immunosuppressed patients. The occurrence of *Pneumocystis* in these 5 previously healthy individuals without a clinically apparent underlying immunodeficiency is unusual. The fact that these patients were all homosexuals suggests an association between some aspect of a homosexual lifestyle or disease acquired through sexual contact and *Pneumocystis* pneumonia in this population.

Morbidity and Mortality Weekly Report, June 5, 1981

E pidemics do not announce themselves but enter on cat's paws. The first cases came before the official start of the AIDS epidemic in June 1981, before the new disease had a name. They came in the form of strange, inexplicable, and untreatable conditions in young men, women, and children. These initial encounters, in the late 1970s, left physicians perplexed, sometimes disturbed. Only gradually, as they told their colleagues about what they had seen and began to hear about other cases, did the realization begin to take hold that something unusual and worrisome was occurring. . . .

Recognizing an Epidemic

Although cases of *Pneumocystis* had begun to appear on both coasts [of the United States], it fell to Michael Gottlieb, a 33-year-old immunologist at UCLA, to bring together the first series that would, when published, mark the official start of the epidemic. In December 1980, as a recently hired assistant professor, Gottlieb was informed by one of his immunology fellows about a gay man with thrush and a low white blood count. Gottlieb immediately detected that "there was something medically interesting about him. He *smelled* like an immune deficiency. You don't get a mouth full of candida without being immune deficient." The man's disclosure of his homosexuality also impressed Gottlieb. "He was on the telephone to a friend one day when we were in the room, and he said to his friend, sort of in jest, 'Hey, yeah, Bruce, the doctors here tell me I am one sick queen!' And we all chuckled because we had very minimal knowledge of the gay community. We weren't familiar with this kind of self-deprecating humor."

On returning from the patient's room, Gottlieb encountered a colleague who was "beginning to fool around with some of the antibodies to T-cell subsets which had just become available as a research tool." At his suggestion, they examined the patient's blood "and found that this man's T-cells were all messed up, that he had virtually no helper T-cells—CD4 cells—and that his CD8 cells, the suppressor cells, were very high."

Soon thereafter, Gottlieb received a call from the chief of rheumatology at Wadsworth VA [Veterans Administration] Hospital in West Los Angeles. He had examined a couple of very sick men, sent to him by Joel Weisman and his colleague, gay physicians with a largely gay practice. Having heard about Gottlieb's patient, he believed that "something interesting" was occurring and wanted to arrange a meeting. Weisman and his partner had already begun to notice unusual diseases in their patients by 1979.

> When you go from relatively healthy people with single system disease—somebody would come in with gonorrhea or diarrhea— [to] seeing multisystem problems, the lymphadenopathies with the fevers, with the funguses, with the rashes [it is striking]. My belief was that you don't have a whole group of people go from having a few problems to a lot of problems. It scared me and I don't scare that easily.

By October 1980, Weisman and his partner had two patients who were very sick with similar conditions: chronic fevers, swollen lymph nodes, diarrhea, and thrush. After Gottlieb and Weisman met in January 1981, Gottlieb tested the T-cells of Weisman's patients and "found the same, now typical, abnormality."

Gottlieb soon had a fourth and a fifth case, all gay men. The fourth case came to Gottlieb through a former student, who was now the Centers for Disease Control (CDC) Epidemic Intelligence Officer in Los Angeles. Michael Gottlieb phoned him to warn him:

> "Something's up. It's in gay men and I think it may have something to do with cytomegalovirus; why don't you see what you can find out?" He said, "Yeah, I'll get right on it." And he went up to the sixth floor of the county health department building, and there was an isolate of cytomegalovirus growing in culture that had been taken from an autopsy of a young man. He decided to look into the case. And he called me the next day and said, "I've reviewed the record. The case is a little more complicated in that the patient had

Hodgkin's Disease 10 years ago and gotten radiation therapy. That might be a predisposing factor for immune deficiency, but he was also gay and he had *Pneumocystis*."

Ultimately, all the cases developed *Pneumocystis carinii* pneumonia. The final case, case number five, came from a Beverly Hills internist who had heard about Gottlieb's experience. Soon thereafter, Gottlieb and the CDC officer began to write up their cases.

[We] met in his apartment and we sat down and we sketched out what became the *Morbidity and Mortality Weekly Report (MMWR)* of June 5, 1981 that reported five patients, all gay men, and it was called "*Pneumocystis* Pneumonia, Los Angeles."

The Report Goes Unnoticed

But what was to become a landmark report went largely unnoticed. Carol Brosgart, a public health doctor in Oakland, California, recalled reading about the five young men and asking herself, What's the malignancy? What's going on here? This is incredible. Probably more representative were the remarks of Neil Schram, a kidney specialist in Los Angeles who would become an AIDS treater and political activist:

Understand, most physicians were absolutely disconnected from the *MMWR*. That was a publication that the CDC put out for the public health people. I had never heard of the CDC; I'd never heard of public health doctors.

His remarks were echoed by Stosh Ostrow, a physician in private practice in Atlanta, who observed, "I wasn't reading the *MMWR* back then; who read the *MMWR?*"

Like physicians, most of the press failed to pick up the *MMWR* story. Two West Coast papers, the *Los Angeles Times* and the *San Francisco Chronicle*, and the Associated Press ran short pieces on the CDC's report. Only when a second *MMWR* appeared on July 3—Alvin Friedman-Kien's description of Kaposi's sarcoma in 26 gay men in New York City and California—was media interest aroused. National Public Radio, the Cable News Network, and the Associated Press ran stories; so did the *New York Times*, with a column-long article headlined "Rare Cancer Seen in 41 Homosexuals." The next day, July 4, 1981, the *Washington Post* followed suit.

At New York Hospital/Cornell Medical Center, an oncologist

interested in viral causes of cancer and viral immunology recalled Gottlieb's article in the *MMWR*, then noted the almost
complete absence of press coverage in its wake. On vacation in
Maine, Jeffrey Laurence read the July 3 *New York Times* report
on Kaposi's sarcoma and thought, "God, now it's come out." Returning to Manhattan the following day, he began to field calls
from gay friends worried about the new gay cancer.

Epidemic Fears

The official early history of AIDS could be told with the headlines
of five articles in *Morbidity and Mortality Weekly Report* that appeared subsequent to those published in June and July 1981:

• July 9, 1982. Opportunistic Infections and Kaposi's Sarcoma
Among Haitians in the United States.

• July 16, 1982. *Pneumocystis Carinii* Pneumonia Among Per-
sons with Hemophilia A.

• December 10, 1982. Possible Transfusion Acquired Immune
Deficiency Syndrome (AIDS)—California.

• December 17, 1982. Unexplained Immunodeficiency and
Opportunistic Infections in Infants.

• January 7, 1983. Immunodeficiency Among Female Sexual
Partners of Males with Acquired Immune Deficiency Syndrome
(AIDS)—New York.

In that 18-month period, the contours of the epidemic as a sexually transmitted, blood-borne disease were made clear, although
the extent of infection in the gay and drug-using population
would not be known until the viral agent responsible for AIDS
was discovered and a blood test developed.

But the landmark reports in *MMWR* tell only the public part
of the story; they do not capture the extent to which those who
first encountered patients with AIDS struggled with the epi-
demiological significance of their clinical experiences, or the extent to which their growing fears of a potentially catastrophic
spread of the new disease met with resistance from colleagues.
Even those who would commit themselves to AIDS work had no
reason to believe initially that a grim clinical picture would produce a grave social burden.

Treating patients with Kaposi's sarcoma in Los Angeles,
Jerome Groopman thought, "This was possibly just an isolated
occurrence in certain areas and would probably be a relatively
unusual disease." Never having seen an AIDS patient, Neil

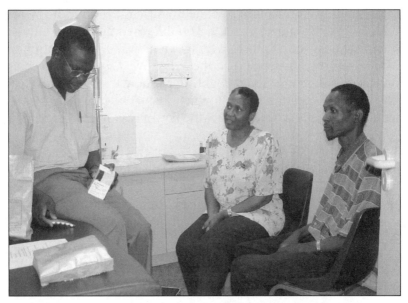

As the first wave of AIDS patients sought treatment, many doctors found themselves discussing sexuality and drug use with their patients.

Schram heard about the new disease at a conference organized by the gay doctors' organization, Bay Area Physicians for Human Rights (BAPHR): "I remember thinking, That's peculiar. It can't mean anything." Fourteen years later, recalling that period, Schram noted sardonically: "I was insightful at the time." Even as late as 1984, when many had become seized with anxiety, infectious disease specialist Stephen Follansbee recalled:

> I think there was certainly the idea that this was a flash in the pan, that this was going to come and go and would die out. I can remember sometime around '83, maybe '84, when we thought actually that cases were dropping off. . . . So therefore this was dying out, and that this was some sort of an epidemic phenomenon that is reproducible in other epidemics where the most vulnerable people get it and die and everyone else develops immunity. That little window of optimism didn't last long.

The Disease Spreads

An error in clinical judgment by many hemophilia specialists had tragic significance for those with bleeding disorders and profound professional consequences for those who had treated them with clotting factor. Margaret Hilgartner, a pioneer who had helped to usher in what some had called "the golden years" of hemophilia treatment, recalled the early response to the first reports of AIDS in those with hemophilia A, the severest form of the disorder:

> Even though this might be the same disease that the gays had, the discussion kept coming into the conversation: Was this going to be like hepatitis? Because if we had 72 percent [infected with hepatitis B], and some clinics had even higher percentages and were surviving, would these patients then survive? Was it going to be as lethal? And if it wasn't going to be lethal like it appeared to be in the gays, did we really have to inform the patients to the same degree and worry about them?

The reluctance to acknowledge the extent to which AIDS would take on epidemic proportions was not unique to the world of hemophilia. Those who already believed that a menacing new disease was taking hold faced what, from the perspective of a few short years later, would seem like sheer blindness. Donna Mildvan, who acknowledged her own failure to recognize AIDS in an intravenous drug user because he wasn't gay, was nevertheless troubled by the resistance she witnessed.

> Everybody was resistant in stages . . . or maybe believed it and couldn't deal with it. I don't know. But it was like nothing was going away; nothing was untrue of our worst fears, and they were just growing, because there would be new fears and new implications, and new populations were getting drawn into this to the point that it had gotten very very awful. . . . The reality was a lot worse than anybody would have ever dreamt.

Dan William, who had worked with Mildvan, was especially concerned about the extent to which the new disease would spread among gay men.

> The anxiety of those early years was palpable. It was very, very much greater than you can describe, because people like Donna and myself, and I think other physicians recognized the potential for the devastation that eventually could ensue. . . . I had very strong feelings about it, and many people didn't want to believe it. If you listen to Jim Curran [head of the CDC's AIDS Program] in

the early days of the epidemic, he always used to end on an optimistic basis, that epidemics come, and they go, so we may be at
the peak, we may not; maybe this is just a little quirk. Keep calm,
and don't be too upset. It was beyond frightening. . . . Realizing
early on that this is probably sexually transmitted, that it's sexually transmitted the same way as hepatitis B, that the prevalence
of hepatitis B in the gay community [may be 40 percent], and the
end result is death or disability, you're talking about a major disaster. . . . History is full of situations like AIDS; it's really not
unique. I mean it's our own holocaust. . . . And [in] every holocaust there were warnings. There was Crystal Night in Germany.

AIDS Becomes a Sexual Issue

For many gay men, a lifestyle involving the broad acceptance
of multiple sexual partners and the thrill of sexual abandon was
part of a precious and newly won freedom. To be told this freedom was implicated in a life-threatening disease was especially
disturbing, even oppressive. To counsel restraint was tantamount
to a rejection of their liberation. In looking back to the first years
of the AIDS epidemic, William Owen, a founding member of
the gay doctors organization, BAPHR was especially concerned
to place gay anxieties in historical perspective and to provide a
justification for those who were circumspect in their warnings
about sex.

It's very easy to look through the retrospectoscope, but the fact of
the matter is that this was a group of people who for many years
had been repressed in terms of their sexuality. And for the first
time in the mid-'70s and after Stonewall in '69, with the dawning
of the gay revolution, people really felt the ability to express themselves sexually, like they couldn't do before; and in some ways it's
like a kid in a candy store. They suddenly had the ability to do
something that they were previously restricted from doing; so
sometimes they go a little bit too far and have too many contacts.
. . . Basically the kind of diseases that we saw people coming in
for were essentially treatable diseases. The gonorrhea was treatable; syphilis was treatable. Giardiasis, shigella infections, they
were all treatable things. If doctors were to have come out then [by
warning about the dangers of an exuberant sexuality], they would
have been seen as some sort of fringe element aligned with either
the church or the state or the psychiatric profession, all of whom

were not held in very high esteem. And so I think our voices would not have been listened to anyway.

While BAPHR did ultimately issue guidelines on sexual risk reduction in 1983, the reaction of many to those who sought to sound the tocsin was dismay. As an openly gay physician, Dan William was especially troubled.

I can remember very vividly; I was scared and anxious and afraid. Not for my own personal safety but for the health of the community. And 95 percent of people were pooh-poohing it. . . . Any kind of intrusion on sexual behavior was looked at as an intrusion upon one's gayness, and that got in the way. And in those early years . . . I got into a little bit of hot water with the community for implying that people had to consider making changes and altering behavior to lessen the probability of transmission of this illness which we did not understand at all.

Resistance to Cautionary Messages

Joseph Sonnabend, whose professional work had involved caring for gay men in New York and who had been especially concerned with sexually transmitted diseases (STDs), suspected that AIDS was the consequence of an immunologic overload, of too many STDs. Although he was skeptical of the notion of contagion, his thesis led to the same behavioral recommendation: radically reduced sexual exposure. The reaction to his urgings was often dismissive. Fifteen years later, he still evidenced a kind of sad perplexity. "I thought I was being of help, but . . . I was being vilified. [I] didn't understand it."

It was the same for Larry Drew in San Francisco, who had been invited to speak in early 1983 by Lea Belli, the wife of attorney Melvin Belli, at their home.

They had a monstrous house on Pacific Avenue, probably the biggest house I'd ever been in, and they devoted the entire upper floor to basically an auditorium, and [I] and three or four others spoke to the group. These were all gay men. [I said] that it was transmissible; that the bathhouse lifestyle was liable to be very important in the transmission. . . . You would have hoped that the reaction was, "Well, gee, thanks for coming and helping us understand this," but the reaction [was], "You're just trying to take away the one recreational activity that we have. You guys all have your golf clubs and tennis clubs, and what have you, and we have the bathhouses. It's just a plot by the straights to screw us again."

But it wasn't just the nonphysician members of the gay community who found the cautionary messages of risk reduction in the face of AIDS difficult to accept. So too did some gay doctors. Even as some like Dan William struggled to convey a message of caution, others continued to embrace denial. Stosh Ostrow describes what may have been the first national conference on AIDS in 1983, a meeting sponsored by the American Association of Physicians for Human Rights and the National Gay and Lesbian Health Education Fund. It was, he recalls, a "horrible meeting."

> The physicians were conservative; the others very radical. We were talking about this disease and lack of government response and blah, blah, blah, and Bernice Goodman got up and said it was a CIA plot to kill the homosexuals. . . . And it was very, very strange, now looking back on it, that we were talking about this disease that was killing people, and [we] knew at that point that it was sexually transmitted but didn't clearly know that we had a responsibility to behave differently. I can remember having sex with another physician there and using Phisohex as a lubricant, thinking, well, it's antibacterial, maybe it'll help. Never considered the idea of a condom.

The focus on gay men made it difficult to recognize that AIDS was also occurring in men who were not exclusively homosexual. In Oakland, California, just across the bay from San Francisco, where the epidemic was taking hold among gay men, Carol Brosgart's first case at a public health clinic for sexually transmitted diseases was bisexual.

> He was a young Black man who said he was bisexual. He was quite poor; he was clearly a prostitute and very open about that. He looked like he had bunches of grapes in each groin and up in the neck and under the arms, just massive lymphadenopathy. The oncologist at the time at the county hospital was very homophobic, so I finally got the surgical resident to do a biopsy on him. And I remember getting a call, and he said, "This is so weird; we got the biopsy results back. The pathologist says it's something called Kaposi's sarcoma [KS]." And right after the first report was the second report of KS in the 26 men in New York, San Francisco, and Los Angeles. He said, "But it's so weird, because it's like this

gay cancer." And I go, "But Steve, he's bisexual," and he says, "Yeah, but this is only in gay men!" He understood there was this new problem, but it had to be in gay men.

In the Bronx, in the summer of 1981, Gerald Friedland, an infectious disease doctor who had recently arrived from Harvard, was asked to consult on three cases, all young men admitted to Montefiore Hospital with *Pneumocystis* pneumonia. In his 15 years as an infectious disease specialist in Africa, the Middle East, and the United States, these were the first cases of PCP he had ever seen—and his first AIDS cases. Well informed about the recent reports of *Pneumocystis* and KS, he automatically assumed that the patients he was to examine were gay men.

> People were talking about these cases, but it was in gay men. So we said to these guys, "You're a gay man, you must be a gay man, come on, admit it." And one guy had an earring.

When the patients still denied being gay, Friedland watched them for further clues and finally established that they were drug users, as they claimed. "I watched to see who visited them, and it was wives and girlfriends and children. It wasn't other gay men. So it look[ed] like it's the same weird disease that doesn't yet have a name, but they're not gay men."

It was not until January 1983 that the CDC directly addressed the issue of the risk to which female partners of men with AIDS were exposed. For Gerald Friedland and his colleagues in the Bronx, recognition of heterosexual transmission of AIDS came sooner.

> We had a few male patients who had female partners. The female partners were not drug users, so if they were at risk it was risk through sexual transmission. . . . And I had one of these sexual partners in clinic, and I'm about to examine her. I put my hands on her neck, and I feel these huge lymph nodes and [I'm thinking], "Oh, shit, she's got it, it's the end of the world." I mean, there are a limited number of gay men in the world, but many, many more heterosexuals. . . . Everything [until then] had been an embellishment, commentary, [but this] to me was a visceral documentation of the fact that it's a heterosexually transmitted disease. . . . This was dread, the end of the world.

Friedland had a dream that gave voice to his fears.

I used to have a dream. . . . Did you ever see *Wild Strawberries?*
There's a scene where the old doctor's walking in a town, and
there's a clock that doesn't have any hands on it, and there's a
hearse that sort of drives off and a coffin falls out. It's very disturbing. So it was similar. And I was walking on Jerome Avenue
[where Montefiore is], this train going overhead, and the green
grocer stalls were all out, and there were a lot of cars and trucks,
but there were no people. They had all died of AIDS. I remember
that dream—I had the sense there was this sort of thing seeping
into the population, and we knew nothing about it, and lots of
people already had it and didn't know about it.

Resistance to the Idea of Heterosexual AIDS

Although Friedland and others had come to recognize that AIDS
could be heterosexually transmitted, there remained a reservoir
of resistance to the idea. Because of his role as a military doctor,
Robert Redfield was particularly interested in the possibility of
such transmission and was struck by the reluctance of others to
acknowledge it.

There was a meeting at Bob Gallo's lab in the fall of 1983, and I
remember there were some CDC representatives, . . . and I remember getting up and presenting the fact that I had five men with
AIDS. . . . And I remember saying it bothered me because three of
the wives have [low T-cell counts]. And I can tell you that most
people just dismissed it. And that kind of frustrated me.

When at last he was able to test for the presence of HIV, his assumption proved correct.

As we got into the cusp of '84, I started actually having viral data
now from Bob's lab, so I knew I was right. And I can tell you,
there was a second of excitement when . . . I was looking at this
stuff. And then I was sick to my stomach. I didn't want to be right.

But even as the possibility of transmission from men to
women was being established, the possibility that women could
transmit disease to men met with resistance. This was especially
so in New York City, where the Department of Health, concerned
about damping AIDS-related hysteria, was particularly skeptical. Donald Kotler, many of whose patients came from Harlem,
was struck by the Health Department's refusals to acknowledge
heterosexually acquired AIDS in men.

What does it take to realize that something is [sexually] transmissible? It's in the gay community. And then to find that it can be transmitted by needles, and it's in the IV drug community. How could it not be? And then to see a woman, and then to see a straight man. The official interpretation is that "a heterosexual man who's not an IV drug user and develops AIDS is defined as a liar." The Department of Health came when I had such a person in the hospital, and that's what they said; they said, "He's a liar. It can't be."

The First Cases of Childhood AIDS

. . . The recognition that AIDS could be transmitted heterosexually emerged concomitantly with the discovery of the new disease in babies. Commenting on four cases of unexplained immunodeficiency and opportunistic infections in infants in New York, New Jersey, and California, the CDC wrote in December 1982, "Transmission of an 'AIDS agent' from mother to child, either in utero or shortly after birth, could account for the early onset of immunodeficiency in these infants." But here too those who first encountered the disease were confronted with what they took to be more than the normal level of scientific skepticism from both professional colleagues and the public health community. Gwendolyn Scott, a pediatric infectious disease specialist at Jackson Memorial, began to see her first cases of children in the same community of patients being seen by Margaret Fischl.

> I saw my first children early in 1981, and they were both under six months of age. They both had mothers who were quite well, at least by appearance, and both of them were very, very sick. Both of them hadn't grown well, so that they were below weight, what we would call "failure to thrive." They were Haitian children. One child had severe oral thrush. She had continuous fever. And she later developed a sepsis, had severe complications, and died before six months of age. The other child had similar problems and she died from a gastrointestinal bleed. They never got out of the hospital. These two children bothered me, because I couldn't decide what they had. So I basically labeled these children as some kind of immune deficiency. It was something I had never seen before. So it was a mystery and an enigma.

. . . Gay men, drug users, blood transfusion recipients, hemophiliacs, the sexual partners of those at risk, and babies born to infected mothers would all be officially diagnosed with AIDS by

June 1984, three years after the first case reports. By then, 4,918 cases had been reported to the CDC; 2,221 were dead. Less than a year later, in May 1985, *MMWR* announced the 10,000th case of AIDS. It had taken three years for the first 5,000 cases to be reported, 10 months for the second 5,000 cases. Those escalating numbers revealed only a small part of the story. The new HIV antibody test, first available for research purposes in 1984, made clear that Gerald Friedland's fear that "this thing was seeping into the population" was all too prescient. Among gay men attending a sexually transmitted disease clinic in San Francisco, the prevalence of antibody to the virus thought to cause AIDS had gone from 1 percent in 1978 to 25 percent in 1980, a year before the first case of AIDS was reported. In 1984, when testing for undiagnosed infection became possible, 65 percent were infected. In New York City, a sample of frequent drug users had an infection rate of 87 percent. Seventy-two percent of asymptomatic hemophiliacs being treated at home had a positive antibody test response.

MTV Changes the Music World

by Carla Hay

When MTV launched its network in August 1981, music videos were not a new phenomenon. Record companies and recording artists, particularly in Great Britain, had been using them to bolster record sales for a number of years. There had even been a number of television shows in Europe and America dedicated solely to airing music videos before MTV entered the market. No one, however, had ever tried to build an entire network around them. Armed with nothing more than a handful of low-budget video clips from English New Wave acts such as Duran Duran and the Buggles, and with incredible market savvy, MTV executives turned the fledgling network into a multimedia juggernaut and, in the process, forever changed music and pop culture.

Though a handful of record labels and musical acts had already been making videos before MTV's debut, few in the industry took the medium seriously. Nowhere was this more evident than in the comic production values of the videos that were made. Most saw them as nothing more than a relatively cheap way to drum up publicity for a certain musical act. As MTV grew in popularity, however, video became indispensable in launching and maintaining a musician's career. Consequently, the bar was raised when it came to quality and budgetary allotment. The early standard by which all videos were judged was Michael Jackson's epic "Thriller." Utilizing Hollywood-style special effects, makeup, and choreography, "Thriller" looked more like a big budget horror film than a music video, and it was an instant hit. The video propelled album sales into the stratosphere, making *Thriller* the highest-selling album of all time. Along with Michael Jackson, MTV launched such acts as Madonna, Guns N' Roses, and Nirvana into superstardom. From the mid-1980s onward, a critic would be hard pressed to name a star act that did not have a video in regular rotation on MTV.

In the following piece Carla Hay, a staff writer for *Billboard* magazine, traces the history of MTV from its inception and early obstacles to its twentieth anniversary in 2001 and the impact it has had on the music industry and on pop culture.

"And to think, they said this wouldn't last." Those were the immortal words uttered by Michael Jackson during an unforgettable MTV moment in which he and then-wife Lisa Marie Presley kissed onstage at the 1994 MTV Video Music Awards. But those words could also apply to MTV, which celebrates its 20th anniversary [in 2001].

The launch date of MTV (Aug. 1, 1981) along with the first video played on MTV (the Buggles' "Video Killed the Radio Star") have become a part of music history. But the struggle to put the network on the air is often overlooked.

Where It All Began

MTV had to overcome the obstacles of finding advertisers when many skeptics thought that a 24-hour music channel on TV wouldn't last beyond a few months. The network also launched at a time when artists rarely made videos, so having enough content to fill the vast programming space was a formidable challenge. (There's an old joke among people who remember the early days of MTV: "How did you get MTV to play your video back then? You made a video.")

Headquartered in New York, MTV, ironically, wasn't even available in that city until a year after its debut. In fact, the network had to celebrate its launch at a restaurant in Fort Lee, N.J.—the closest place to New York that aired MTV at the time.

Twenty years later, few can deny that MTV has become more than a music channel. It's become the world's largest TV network, an influential force in pop culture and one of the most recognizable brand names in the world.

According to MTV, the network is in more than 342 million

households around the world (including over 78 million in the U.S.), and [2000] was MTV's highest-rated year to date. Ratings for first-quarter 2001 have jumped 20% compared to the same period last year. In addition, MTV Networks' pro forma revenues of $3 billion [in 2000] (up 14% from the previous year) were largely due to MTV, whose advertising revenues are expected to be about $700 million [in 2001].

In celebration of its first two decades, MTV will be televising a 20th-anniversary concert, set to take place Aug. 1, [2001] at New York's Hammerstein Ballroom.

MTV Networks chairman/CEO Tom Freston says, "To say that MTV has in any way changed the music industry would be kind of arrogant. But we did make the music industry more cognizant of TV, and we helped the industry get a finger on the pulse of what people are interested in."

"Sometimes MTV gets too much credit for things," says Judy McGrath, president of the MTV Group and chairman of Interactive Music. "But we've gotten one thing right: We've done a pretty good job of reflecting the needs of fans. It feels like MTV lets the audience own the network."

Nielsen Media Research consistently ranks MTV as the No. 1 cable network among 12- to 34-year-olds—MTV's target audience, which McGrath says is currently the "most marketed-to, most diverse, open-minded generation that has ever existed."

The First Airing

The origins of MTV can be traced back to many people, but it was Warner American Express Satellite Entertainment Company (WASEC) executive John Lack—inspired by *Popclips*, a must-video show created in the late '70s by Michael Nesmith of the Monkees—who is given a great deal of credit for helping the dream become a reality.

The industry first heard about WASEC's plans for a 24-hour music channel when Lack announced it at the 1979 Billboard Music Video Conference. He—along with other WASEC executives Jack Schneider, Bob McGroarty and Bob Pittman (now co-COO of AOL Time Warner)—set in motion the network that would become MTV. WASEC officially approved the network in January 1981.

Although Nesmith declined to be a part of MTV, WASEC wasted no time in assembling a group that would become MTV's first pioneering executive team, including Freston, John Sykes (now president of VH1 and CMT), Steve Casey, Sue Steinberg, Carolyn Baker and Fred Seibert. McGrath was also part of MTV's original staff.

Less than nine months later, MTV was born, at 12:01 A.M. on Aug. 1, 1981.

The second video to be played on MTV was Pat Benatar's "You Better Run." Benatar remembers vividly the first time she saw MTV: "The day MTV started, my band and I were in Oklahoma for this festival called Rocklahoma. The hotel had a feed of MTV, and we waited anxiously for the moment it came on. They played 'Your Better Run' every 20 minutes, and we sat there stunned for at least an hour. Within a week of being on MTV, I couldn't go anywhere without being recognized."

Benatar is considered by many to be the first female solo artist to become a major MTV star. Of this, she says, "I can't emphasize enough what MTV did for me and my career. MTV broke down a lot of barriers. Back then, rock radio discriminated against women—they wouldn't play more than one female singer within a certain time period. But MTV didn't care if you were female, or how many other female artists they were playing. That's what made MTV a maverick, and eventually radio caught up."

Helping Make Superstars

"I grew up on MTV, so I consider myself part of the first MTV generation," says Jordan Schur, president of Geffen Records and founder of Flip Records. "MTV has been one of the essential places I've gone to for music. Presented the right way, MTV can do tremendous things for artists, and I've seen the results happen for our bands after MTV got involved."

Schur—who works with such artists as Limp Bizkit, Weezer, Beck, Guns N' Roses and Staind—adds, "MTV does its best to understand the artists and present the artists' visions the way they want them to be presented."

Staind lead singer Aaron Lewis notes, "Getting exposure on MTV is really the best advertising that money can't buy."

One of the first bands to benefit directly from MTV exposure before receiving mainstream radio airplay was Duran Duran. The group's founder/keyboardist Nick Rhodes attributes much of Duran Duran's audience growth in the U.S. to MTV. "MTV and Duran Duran arrived around the same time, so our timing was immaculate," he says. "Music videos were fairly new at the time, so it was like a blank canvas that we could fill with this art form." Lead singer Simon LeBon adds, "The power for artists to be in people's homes visually had a lot to do with MTV."

Veteran artist Sammy Hagar—whose solo career and 10-year stint in Van Halen have received considerable exposure on MTV—says of the impact the network had on his life: "Before MTV, most of the people who would recognize you in public would be your fans. I remember once MTV started playing my [1983] video for 'Three Lock Box,' I started getting recognized everywhere by people who might not necessarily be into my music. It blew my mind."

Mary J. Blige remembers, "I found out about MTV when I was in junior high, when they were playing a lot of Michael Jackson and Duran Duran. There's no question that a lot of people can become big stars once their video hits MTV."

Michael Jackson's 1983 videos from his landmark *Thriller* album ("Billie Jean," "Beat It" and the epic "Thriller," which premiered on MTV) are considered by many to be watershed moments for MTV by opening the door for more African-American artists to be played on the network. Jackson's state-of-the-art videos are also viewed as the first to raise the stakes on music-video budgets.

MTV/MTV2 and MTV Films president Van Toffler says, "Michael Jackson's 'Thriller' video really made people stand up and take notice. Suddenly, Hollywood started invading our coffers for ideas, on-camera talent and off-camera talent."

Mark on Pop Culture

Daryl Hall of Hall & Oates says, "Music became a different animal after MTV. Videos went from simple things that hardly any artist wanted to do to overblown insanity. Hall & Oates benefited from MTV not just because of our music but because we happened to be photogenic people."

"MTV has made artists think more visually," observes Toffler. "I've heard artists talk about their future albums, and, before the songs are even recorded, they're talking about what the video is going to look like."

"MTV has twice as much of an effect for artists than radio, because there's that visual element," says Slash, a former member of Guns N' Roses, whose videos (including "November Rain" and "Sweet Child O' Mine") are often ranked among the most popular MTV videos of all time. "It's always a huge crapshoot for a new artist to have a hit, but most struggling artists see heavy rotation on MTV as being one of the pinnacles of success."

Whether MTV has been credited with influencing TV, feature films and—for better or worse—the way artists express themselves, the network's growth in its first two decades has been rapid and filled with notable changes, including being purchased by Viacom in 1985.

In an informal Billboard survey, numerous music-industry professionals, including artists, named several outstanding MTV landmarks that had dramatic effects on the music industry. These landmarks include the annual MTV Video Music Awards, which bowed in 1984; MTV's coverage of Live Aid (July 13, 1985), which many say established MTV as a powerful news source for music; MTV's annual New Year's Eve celebration, which began in 1981; MTV's first international launch in 1987 with MTV Europe and MTV Australia; MTV showing directors' credits on videos, beginning in 1992; and the MTV series *Unplugged, 120 Minutes, Headbanger's Ball, Yo! MTV Raps* and *Total Request Live (TRL)*.

Branching Out

"*TRL* has become the Holy Grail of pop music," says Universal Records senior VP of promotion Steve Leeds, who worked in studio operations at MTV in the late '80s. "*Yo! MTV Raps* was also one of the most important things MTV did, because it brought hip-hop culture to mainstream America. The MTV Video Music Awards are also important, because it brought an edge to awards shows that we'd never seen before on TV."

Def Jam Records founder/music mogul Russell Simmons adds, "There is always a noticeable increase in an artist's sales whenever MTV plays that person's video. MTV has always been creative and interesting. When BET wouldn't play rap, MTV did. MTV changed the way we look at TV and music. And MTV has the best music-awards show on TV, period."

"MTV has broken down the walls between the artist and the audience," says Joey McIntyre, formerly of New Kids on the Block and now a solo artist who has made frequent guest appearances on *TRL*. "MTV is also more personality-driven now than it was in the '80s. MTV has Hollywood-ized the music industry, because many of the artists on MTV have become in demand in Hollywood."

Mandy Moore, a hit singer who is also a VJ on MTV, notes, "When my first single, 'Candy,' was released, it did OK. But then it started getting a lot of requests on *TRL*, and then radio followed and started playing the song even more. I have MTV to thank for that and so much of what I've been able to achieve."

Over the years, MTV has ventured into non-music programming that includes game shows, reality programs, cartoons, public-service programs, comedy shows and soap operas. This change in MTV's direction has gotten a mixed reaction, with much of the criticism coming from the music industry.

McGrath says, "A lot of the music industry is still focused on [video] spins on MTV—looking at MTV the same way they look at radio—instead of seeing the value of [MTV shows] *Making the Video* or *Cribs*, or the artist doing something on MTV that connects with the audience. It's been a long process to get the industry to not be so focused on the quantity of videos that are played."

Perhaps to satisfy those with an appetite for 24-hour music-video programming, MTV launched spinoffs MTV2 (originally named M2) in 1996 and MTV X (hard rock/heavy metal) and MTV S (Latin music) in 1998. All three spinoffs are available primarily through digital cable or satellite TV.

But, in terms of size and influence, few would argue that MTV, the original network, still remains the king of all music-video channels. And MTV executives say that music and music videos will remain the heart and soul of MTV.

As McGrath concludes, "Videos add to the experience of music, and, even though some videos have a [sameness] to their quality, I think highly of the art form. It's better than watching regular television."

3

The IBM Personal Computer Debuts:
August 12, 1981

IBM Dominates the PC Market

by Martin Campbell-Kelly and William Aspray

The personal computer (PC) was not born when IBM introduced its own version on August 12, 1981, as much as it was legitimized. PCs had existed since the mid-1970s, but they were only known to a handful of dedicated electronics hobbyists, and few people saw the need to ever use, much less buy, one. This was due in part to the fact that the first PCs were prohibitively expensive and crudely designed (many lacked such basic amenities as floppy drives, power supplies, monitors, and keyboards). The other reason that the PC did not catch on with the public was the absence of relevant software. Other than games, few programs were available that would make the PC of use to anyone in a personal or business setting. This made the PC nothing more than a very expensive calculator or toy. By 1980, however, dozens of spreadsheet and word-processing programs had been developed and sold, and many traditional business machine manufacturers like IBM began to see the PC's potential as a business tool.

To the casual observer, it may have looked as if IBM watched passively from the sidelines as upstart companies like Apple and Commodore seized control of the PC market in the late 1970s. With the rise of popular business-related software, however, the corporate giant sprang into action. In the fall of 1980 IBM approved a prototype, and less than a year later IBM personal computers were rolling off the assembly lines and into stores. The presence of the IBM logo assured many skeptics that the PC was a viable business tool, and the IBM model became so popular that production could

---

Martin Campbell-Kelly and William Aspray, *Computer: A History of the Information Machine*. New York: BasicBooks, 1996, pp. 253–58. Copyright © 1996 by Martin Campbell-Kelly and William Aspray. Reproduced by permission.

not keep pace with demand. IBM had to quadruple production, and in many cases, customers still had to be placed on waiting lists. The IBM PC did much more than dominate the nascent PC market, it became the industry standard. The IBM PC spawned an entire subindustry of clone machines and companies dedicated to manufacturing IBM-compatible peripherals and add-ons. The companies that did not adapt to the IBM standard soon found themselves out of business.

In the following essay Martin Campbell-Kelly and William Aspray trace the history of the IBM PC and its impact on the computer industry. Martin Campbell-Kelly is a reader in computer science at the University of Warwick in Coventry, England. William Aspray is professor of informatics at Indiana University, Bloomington. They are coauthors of *Computer: A History of the Information Machine*, from which the following essay is excerpted.

I BM was not, in fact, the giant that slept soundly during the personal-computer revolution. IBM had a sophisticated market research organization that attempted to predict market trends. The company was well aware of microprocessors and personal computers. Indeed, in 1975 it had developed a desktop computer for the scientific market (the model 5100), but it did not sell well. By 1980 IBM was selling a dedicated word processor based on microprocessor technology. But its sales came a poor second to its traditional electric typewriters, of which IBM was still selling a million a year.

Once the personal computer became clearly defined as a business machine in 1980, IBM reacted with surprising speed. The proposal that IBM should enter the personal-computer business came from William C. Lowe, a senior manager who headed the company's "entry-level systems" in Boca Raton, Florida. In July 1980 Lowe made a presentation to IBM's senior management in Armonk, New York, with a radical plan: Not only should IBM enter the personal-computer market but it should also abandon its traditional development processes in order to match the dynamism of the booming personal-computer industry.

For nearly a century IBM had operated a bureaucratic development process by which it typically took three years for a new product to reach the market. Part of the delay was due to IBM's century-old vertical integration practice, by which it maximized profits by manufacturing in-house all the components used in its products: semiconductors, switches, plastic cases, and so on. Lowe argued that IBM should instead adopt the practice of the rest of the industry by outsourcing all the components it did not already have in production, including software. Lowe proposed yet another break with tradition—that IBM should not use its direct sales force to sell the personal computer but should instead use regular retail channels.

Surprisingly, in light of its stuffy image, IBM's top management agreed to all that Lowe recommended, and within two weeks of his presentation he was authorized to go ahead and build a prototype, which had to be ready for the market within twelve months. The development of the personal computer would be known internally as Project Chess.

IBM's relatively late entry into the personal computer market gave it some significant advantages. First, it could make use of the second generation of microprocessors (which processed sixteen bits of data at a time instead of eight); this would make the IBM personal computer significantly faster than any other machine on the market. IBM chose to use the Intel 8088 chip, thereby guaranteeing Intel's future prosperity.

The IBM personal computer dominated the market and became the industry standard in the early 1980s.

Although IBM was the world's largest software developer, paradoxically it did not have the skills to develop software for personal computers. Its bureaucratic software development procedures were slow and methodical, and geared to large software artifacts; the company lacked the critical skills needed to develop the "quick-and-dirty" software needed for personal computers.

IBM initially approached Gary Kildall of Digital Research— the developer of the CP/M operating system—for operating software for the new computer, and herein lies one of the more poignant stories in the history of the personal computer. For reasons now muddied, Kildall blew the opportunity. One version of the story has it that he refused to sign IBM's nondisclosure agreement, while another version has him doing some recreational flying while the dark-suited IBMers cooled their heels below. In any event, the opportunity passed Digital Research by and moved on to Microsoft. Over the next decade, buoyed by the revenues from its operating system for the IBM personal computer, Microsoft became the quintessential business success story of the late twentieth century, and Bill Gates became a billionaire at the age of thirty-one. Hence, for all of Gates's self-confidence and remarkable business acumen, he owes almost everything to being in the right place at the right time.

The IBM entourage arrived at Bill Gates and Paul Allen's Microsoft headquarters in July 1980. It was then a tiny (thirty-two-person) company located in rented offices in downtown Seattle. It is said that Gates and Allen were so keen to win the IBM contract that they actually wore business suits and ties. Although Gates may have appeared a somewhat nerdish twenty-nine-year-old who looked fifteen, he came from an impeccable background, was palpably serious, and showed a positive eagerness to accommodate the IBM culture. For IBM, he represented as low a risk as any of the personal-computer software firms, almost all of which were noted for their studied contempt for Big Blue. It is said that when John Opel, IBM's president, heard about the Microsoft deal, he said, "Is he Mary Gates's son?" He was. Opel and Gates's mother both served on the board of the United Way.

At the time that Microsoft made its agreement with IBM for an operating system, it did not have an actual product, nor did it have the resources to develop one in IBM's time scale. However, Gates obtained a suitable piece of software from a local software firm, Seattle Computer Products, for $30,000 cash. Eventually, the operating system, known as MS-DOS, would be bundled with almost every IBM personal computer and compatible machine, earning Microsoft a royalty of between $10 and $50 on every copy sold.

By the fall of 1980 the prototype personal computer, known internally as the Acorn, was complete; IBM's top management gave final authorization to go into production. Up to this point the Acorn had been only a development project like any other—now serious money was involved. Lowe, his mission essentially accomplished, moved up into the higher echelons of IBM, leaving his second-in-command, Don Estridge, in overall charge. Estridge was an unassuming forty-two-year-old. Although, as the corporate spokesman for the IBM personal computer, he later became as well known as any IBMer apart from the company's president, he never attracted as much media attention as the Young Turks such as Gates and Steve Jobs.

The development team under Estridge was now increased to more than a hundred, and factory arrangements were made for IBM to assemble computers using largely outsourced components. Contracts for the bulk supply of subsystems were finalized with Intel for the 8088 microprocessor, with Tandon for floppy disk drives, with Zenith for power supplies, and with the Japanese company Epson for printers. Contracts were also firmed up for software. Besides Microsoft for its operating system and BASIC, arrangements were made to develop a version of the VisiCalc spreadsheet, a word processor, and a suite of business programs. A games program, Adventure, was also included with the machine, suggesting that even at this late date it was not absolutely clear whether the personal computer was a domestic machine, a business machine, or both.

Not everyone in IBM was happy to see the personal computer—whether for home or business—in the company's product line. One insider was reported as saying:

> Why on earth would you care about the personal computer? It has nothing at all to do with office automation. It isn't a product for big companies that use "real" computers. Besides, nothing much may come of this and all it can do is cause embarrassment to IBM, because, in my opinion, we don't belong in the personal computer business to begin with.

Overriding these pockets of resistance inside the company,

IBM began to actively consider marketing. The economics of the personal computer determined that it could not be sold by IBM's direct sales force because the profit margins would be too slender. The company negotiated with the Chicago-based Sears Company to sell the machine at its Business Centers and contracted with ComputerLand to retail the machine in its stores. For its traditional business customers, IBM would also sell the machines in its regular sales offices, alongside office products such as electric typewriters and word processors.

Early in 1981, only six months after the inception of Project Chess, IBM appointed the West Coast–based Chiat Day advertising agency to develop an advertising campaign. Market research suggested that the personal computer still lay in the gray area between regular business equipment and a home machine. The advertising campaign was therefore ambiguously aimed at both the business and home user. The machine was astutely named the IBM Personal Computer, suggesting that the IBM machine and the personal computer were synonymous. For the business user, the fact that the machine bore the IBM logo was sufficient to legitimate it inside the corporation. For the home user, however, market research revealed that although the personal computer was perceived as a good thing, it was also seen as intimidating—and IBM itself was seen as "cold and aloof." The Chiat Day campaign attempted to allay these fears by featuring in its advertisements a Charlie Chaplin lookalike and alluding to Chaplin's famous movie *Modern Times.* Set in a futuristic automated factory, *Modern Times* showed the "little man" caught up in a world of hostile technology, confronting it, and eventually overcoming it. The Charlie Chaplin figure reduced the intimidation factor and gave IBM "a human face."

During the summer of 1981 the first machines began to come off the IBM assembly plant in Boca Raton, and by early August initial shipments totaling 1,700 machines had been delivered to Sears Business Centers and ComputerLand stores ready for the launch. A fully equipped IBM Personal Computer, with 64 Kbytes of memory and a floppy disk, cost $2,880.

The IBM Personal Computer was given its press launch in New York on 12 August. There was intense media interest, which generated many headlines in the computer and business press. In the next few weeks the IBM Personal Computer became a runaway success that exceeded almost everyone's expectations, inside and outside the company. While many business users had hesitated over whether to buy an Apple or a Commodore or a Tandy machine, the presence of the IBM logo convinced them that the technology was for real: IBM had legitimated the personal computer. There was such a demand for the machine that production could not keep pace, and retailers could do no more than placate their customers by placing their names on a waiting list. Within days of the launch, IBM decided to quadruple production.

During 1982–83 the IBM Personal Computer became an industry standard. Most of the popular software packages were converted to run on the machine, and the existence of this software reinforced its popularity. This encouraged other manufacturers to produce "clone" machines, which ran the same software. This was very easy to do because the Intel 8088 microprocessor used by IBM and almost all the other subsystems was readily available on the open market. Among the most successful of the clone manufacturers was Houston-based Compaq, which produced its first machine in 1982. In its first full year of business, it achieved sales of $110 million. Adroitly swimming with the tide, several of the leading manufacturers such as Tandy, Commodore, Victor, and Zenith switched into making IBM-compatible products. Alongside the clone manufacturers, a huge subindustry developed to manufacture peripherals, memory boards, and add-ons. The software industry published thousands of programs for the IBM-compatible personal computer—or the IBM PC, as the machine soon became known. In 1983 it was estimated that there were a dozen monthly magazines and a score of weekly newspapers for users of the machine. Most famously, in January 1983, the editors of *Time* magazine nominated as their Man of the Year not a person but a machine: the PC.

Almost all the companies that resisted the switch to the IBM standard soon went out of existence or were belatedly forced into conforming. The only important exception was Apple Computer, whose founder, Steve Jobs, had seen another way to compete with the IBM standard: not by making cheaper hardware but by making better software.

A Nuclear Reactor at Chernobyl Melts Down: April 26, 1986

The Impact of Chernobyl

by Fred Pearce

In the early morning of April 26, 1986, a scheduled test of the number four reactor at the Chernobyl nuclear power plant in the Soviet Ukraine went horribly wrong. A series of powerful explosions rocked the station, and in an instant fifty tons of evaporated nuclear fuel spewed thirty-six thousand feet into the air. It took Soviet fire crews ten days to get the fires under control. In that time, a core meltdown sent a plume over the surrounding area that contained as much as one hundred times the radiation of the atomic bombs dropped on Hiroshima and Nagasaki. Within forty-eight hours the cloud reached Sweden and continued to spread over Europe. Radiation leakage was finally stopped when a massive concrete sarcophagus was built over the destroyed reactor. Irreparable damage, however, had already been done.

Although the official death toll from the accident stands at thirty-two, few have solid numbers to indicate what the long-term effects of radiation exposure will bring for the population in the immediate area and in Europe. Soviet secrecy at the time of the accident (no public mention of the disaster was made for at least ten days, and even then, details were vague) has contributed to the difficulty in determining the extent of the damage. In the following years a dramatic increase in cancer, birth defects, and animal mutations has been observed in Belarus, Ukraine, Russia, and the Baltics. Some Ukrainian estimates put the eventual death toll at fifteen thousand. Moreover, entire cities were rendered uninhabitable, hundreds of thousands of people were displaced, and huge tracts of land were

Fred Pearce, "Chernobyl: The Political Fallout Continues," *UNESCO Courier*, October 2000. Copyright © 2000 by United Nations Education, Scientific, and Cultural Organization. Reproduced by permission.

rendered unfit for agriculture for as long as three hundred years. Some, however, for lack of another place to go, still live and farm in areas that are highly contaminated.

In the following essay Fred Pearce, an environmental journalist and consultant for the British weekly *New Scientist*, documents the damage and the ongoing difficulty in determining accurate figures in the wake of the Chernobyl accident.

A sigh of relief ripples across Europe as engineers prepare to shut down Chernobyl, the world's most feared nuclear power plant, on December 15, [2000]. Politicians have finally brokered a deal in which Western donors foot the bill of about two billion dollars to close and fully entomb the Ukrainian reactors. Yet for many ordinary citizens, the nightmare continues. . . .

On April 26, [2000,] thousands marched solemnly through the towns of Belarus, Ukraine and eastern Russia to commemorate the dead from the nuclear disaster 14 years before. At 1:26 AM bells tolled to mark the moment when a Chernobyl reactor blew and a deadly radioactive fall-out began to blanket their fields and towns. But as well as mourning, there was fear. Fear of the continuing radiation, which could claim thousands more. And fear of speaking out of turn. That night, Yuri Bandazhevsky, rector of the Gomel Medical Institute in Belarus until his arrest [in 1999], was forced into internal exile in the capital of Minsk. He is one of many researchers who say their work has been suppressed or ignored by governments anxious to play down the radiation risks their citizens still face.

Estimates of the death toll to date range from the 32 offered by UN nuclear scientists to the 15,000 suggested by some Ukrainian researchers. In June [2000,] scientists at the UN's Scientific Committee on the Effects of Atomic Radiation (UNSCEAR) reported that "there is no evidence of a major public health impact attributable to radiation, apart from a high level of thyroid cancer in children [from which] few should die." Yet the previous day the UN Secretary-General, Kofi Annan, appeared to disagree when he said: "The catastrophe is far from over. It continues to have a devastating effect not only on the health of the people, but on every aspect of society." So what is the truth? And how do these disparities arise?

The accident at the Chernobyl nuclear power plant reduced the Number Four reactor to an inferno spewing out a radioactive cloud for ten days. It released a hundred times more radioactivity than the atomic bombs at Hiroshima and Nagasaki combined. For several days there was total silence, before the panic evacuation of some 116,000 people from an exclusion zone that stretched up to 30 kilometres from the plant.

Only years after the accident did the public learn that a larger zone some 150 kilometres away near the Belarus town of Gomel and extending into Russia suffered heavy fall-out in rain shortly after the accident. It emerged in 1989 that a fifth of Belarus had been significantly contaminated. Some 400,000 people were re-settled. And today around four million people still live in areas with some acknowledged contamination.

Official secrecy inside the Soviet Union and its successor governments about the extent of the contamination continues to bedevil the task of keeping people safe, says Greenpeace's Chernobyl specialist Tobias Muenchmeyer. Researchers inside the affected countries agree. "A regime of secrecy was accepted in our country from the very first second the catastrophe happened," says Vladimir Chernousenko, the Ukrainian scientist who coordinated the post-accident clean-up.

A partial information blackout by governments, combined with scientific caution, has helped lead UN agencies into seriously underestimating the death toll, Muenchmeyer believes. Critics of the nuclear industry such as Rosalie Bertell, president of the International Institute of Concern for Public Health in Toronto, say there is another political reason. They point to a 1959 agreement between the International Atomic Energy Agency (IAEA) and the World Health Organization (WHO), which said that "the IAEA had the primary responsibility for encouraging, assisting and co-ordinating research on, and the development and practical application of atomic energy." According to Bertell, "the IAEA has since considered itself to be the watchdog over information about radiation health effects which is distributed to the public." Bertell and other organizations . . . called for the WHO to amend the agreement [in 2000]. The most important radioactive isotopes released at Chernobyl were iodine and caesium. Iodine-131 has a half-life (the time it takes for half the atoms of a radioactive isotope to decay) of eight days. It was mostly inhaled and eaten in contaminated food. Caesium-137 has a half-life of some 30 years. It is still present in soils and vegetation and continues to contaminate people through foodstuff. Some lesser isotopes have half-lives of hundreds or even thousands of years.

Controversy over the Casualty List

Who suffered? In the front line were the "liquidators"—the estimated 600,000 to 800,000 soldiers and public employees drafted in to make the reactor safe and bury contaminated waste. Some 50,000 of them worked on top of the reactor. "They were supposed to stay on the roof to fight the fire for only 90 seconds, then be replaced. One can easily guess this did not happen," says Jean-Pierre Revel, senior health official at the International Federation of the Red Cross. As a result, 237 liquidators were hospitalized; 32 died.

But since then, the Soviet Union and its successors have been unable or unwilling to keep track of this most-at-risk group. According to Leonid Ilyin, a former Russian member of the International Commission on Radiological Protection, "none of these men was registered by name. None was checked [for subsequent health] on a regular basis. They all went back to their homes." This failure is probably the largest organizational cause of the disputes over Chernobyl's death toll. [In] April [1999], Viacheslav Grishin, president of the Chernobyl League—a Kiev-based organization that claims to represent the liquidators—said 15,000 liquidators had died and 50,000 were handicapped. His source was a controversial estimate by Chernousenko, based on likely cancer rates from radiation doses that he believes the liquidators received.

Cancers have been the biggest long-term medical fear. By 1991, doctors were reporting many cases of thyroid cancer among children under four at the time of the disaster. In 1992, a group of Western researchers, including Keith Baverstock of the WHO, agreed that Chernobyl was the likely cause. Yet it was only in 1995, after some 800 cases had emerged, that the UN system formally accepted the finding. This delay had serious implications in finding and treating the disease, which is not fatal if caught early enough.

Playing Politics and Crushing Dissent

The conclusion had been initially controversial partly because the evidence from Hiroshima and Nagasaki suggested that there should be far fewer cases. But politics also entered the equation. The *Economist* magazine speculated that "if the health risks have been underestimated or understated, the American government could face new lawsuits on everything from the Nevada [nuclear] tests to the Three Mile Island nuclear accident in 1979."

At any rate, there are now some 1,800 recorded cases of thyroid cancer attributed to Chernobyl. In the most contaminated districts, such as Gomel, childhood rates are 200 times those in western Europe. Estimates of the total number of cases expected to arise in the future range from a "few thousand," suggested by the IAEA, to the 66,000 predicted for a single group—Belarusian children under four at the time of the disaster—by WHO scientist Elisabeth Cardis, who stressed that "the risk estimates are very uncertain."

What about other cancers which take longer to develop? Officially, the WHO stands by its assessment of 1996 that while "there have been some reports of increases in the incidence of specific malignancies in some populations living in contaminated territories and in liquidators, these reports are not consistent and could reflect differences in the follow-up of exposed populations." But some of its scientists are sceptical. They ask not what can be proved, but what can be expected on the basis of known science. Based on Hiroshima and Nagasaki, Baverstock expects an "excess" of some 6,600 fatal cancers, including 470 leukaemia cases. But a team of Belarusian doctors claims to have found leukaemia rates four times the national average among heavily exposed liquidators. And there are fears that, as with thyroid cancer, rates could be far higher than expected.

But scientific uncertainty should not detract from the fact that there are political reasons why the truth about the disaster may remain hidden, says Muenchmeyer of Greenpeace. National governments, who act as gatekeepers for most of the statistics reaching UN agencies, have a political agenda, he says. The Ukraine is running 14 nuclear reactors with another four under construction, according to the IAEA. "So the Ukraine doesn't want to ruin the image of nuclear power by stressing the harm done by Chernobyl," says Muenchmeyer, "but they also want aid for health programmes. So then they are interested in showing the burden. Often they contradict themselves within a few days."

The Belarus government has consistently downplayed the disaster, even though the country received an estimated 70 per cent of the fall-out. "They decided that the territory and the number of people affected are so great, and the government so poor, that they cannot solve the problem. They decided to shut down dissent," says Muenchmeyer. This has hampered research and apparently prevented findings by local scientists from reaching UN agencies.

Two years ago, Rosa Goncharova of the Institute of Genetics and Cytology in Minsk reported evidence that congenital abnormalities were turning up in the children of those irradiated by Chernobyl. She told a conference that since 1985, cases of cleft palate, Down's syndrome and other deformities had increased by 83 per cent in the areas most heavily contaminated, 30 per cent in moderately contaminated areas and 24 per cent in "clean" areas. But two years later, when contacted for this article, Cardis of the WHO said she had "not received copies of the paper" by Goncharova. Nor had she received copies of work by the director of the independent Belarusian Institute of Radiation Safety (Belrad), Vasily Nesterenko. He had found that in the most contaminated areas, the incidence of diseases of the circulatory system had risen fourfold and deaths among children from respiratory diseases were up 14-fold.

The Dangers of the Twilight Zone

And consider the fate of Yuri Bandazhevsky, whose case has been taken up by Amnesty International. As rector of the Gomel Medical Institute, he carried out autopsies at the city's forensic morgue, on bodies whose deaths were not considered connected to Chernobyl. He examined their internal organs and compared them to the organs of rats that he had fed grain containing radioactive caesium. He was shocked by his findings: "The pathological modifications of the kidneys, heart, liver and lungs was identical to those among the experimental rats." From this he concluded, "that accumulation of radiocaesium in the organs played a major role in the triggering of pathological responses." In other words, it made them ill and even killed them.

His paper went ignored. His subsequent criticism of the post-Chernobyl research conducted by the Ministry of Health brought him more enemies. And last summer he was arrested on unspecified bribery charges, and locked up for six months. His computer and all his files were confiscated and he remains confined to Minsk "under investigation." People are still being exposed to radiation from Chernobyl. In large areas of Belarus in particular the environment is still heavily contaminated. The WHO says "some foods produced by private farmers do exceed [WHO limits]." But it points out that most large farms minimize take-up of radioactivity in soils by deep ploughing and applying fertilizers. "No food produced by collective farms now exceeds the limits." But thousands of people rely on private farms, according to Belrad's Nesterenko, who maintains that a quarter of the food grown inside the contaminated zone supersedes official radioactivity limits. More than 500 villages are drinking contaminated milk. Moreover, many people rely on "wild" produce such as mushrooms, berries and hunted meat—the most risky food of all says the WHO's Baverstock. And, of course, there are the people who return to live a twilight life inside the exclusion zone, replanting their contaminated gardens, gathering food from the forests and raiding abandoned food stores. Most are old women, who judged that the radioactivity could do them little harm at their age. But there are recent unconfirmed reports of a baby being born there. The tragedy, as Kofi Annan said, goes on.

A Russian Journalist Recalls April 26, 1986

by Alla Yaroshinskaya

On April 26, 1986, a reactor at the Chernobyl nuclear power plant in the Soviet Ukraine exploded. The accident resulted in the worst nuclear disaster in history. The ensuing meltdown spewed tons of radioactive material over the surrounding countryside and created a radioactive cloud that soon spread out over Europe and drifted into the Western Hemisphere. What made matters worse for many of the people living in the general vicinity of Chernobyl was the Soviet government's efforts to keep the accident a secret. Official word of the accident was not given until ten days after the reactor exploded. In the following essay, Alla Yaroshinskaya, a Russian journalist who lived in a town that neighbored the Chernobyl plant, explains that the people in the area had no idea of what was happening just a few dozen miles away. Yaroshinskaya recalls how people went about their daily routines on that spring day completely unaware that they were being exposed to extremely high doses of radiation. Yaroshinskaya also describes the sense of panic that began to spread when the rumors of the accident began to filter into the surrounding towns. She eventually learned of the disaster from foreign radio stations and tried in vain to move her family away from the area. The following account is excerpted from Yaroshinskaya's book, *Chernobyl: The Forbidden Truth*.

Alla Yaroshinskaya, *Chernobyl: The Forbidden Truth*, translated by Michel Kahn and Julia Sallabank. Lincoln: University of Nebraska Press, 1995. Copyright © 1995 by the University of Nebraska Press. Reproduced by permission.

My family lives in Zhitomir, a small forest town in the Ukraine. It's a very old Slavic land, where the first traces of human presence date from as long ago as two thousand BC. My ancestors tilled this land in the bronze age, and at the beginning of the iron age. As witnesses we have tombs and the remains of an ancient Russian town.

Zhitomir was first mentioned in the Chronicles in 1392. It is said that the town was named after its founder, a warrior under the Russian princes Alexander and Dir. The name is formed from two words, *zhito* and *mir*, which in Ukrainian mean 'rye' and 'peace'. Thus the town's name encapsulates a whole philosophy of life, which all people can understand.

At the centre of the town is the Castle Mount. According to tradition, this is where the town began. On this hill, bathed on one side by the waters of the River Kamianka, and on the other by the River Teterev, a fort was built. The town grew beside it, inhabited by artisans, blacksmiths, potters, hunters, farmers and merchants. The thick forests which surrounded Zhitomir were rich in game, wild fruits, mushrooms and edible roots. The rivers on whose steep banks the town was built teemed with fish. With a mysterious, infallible talent, our ancestors chose the most enchanting places to build their towns and temples. For eternity.

The surrounding area has kept its beauty; every walk reveals new marvels. Just a few kilometres from Zhitomir, you find yourself in the heart of virgin countryside: the Teterev, whose clear waters flow between enormous blocks of stone, the forest on both banks, the rocks covered with moss and trees, the gorges, and in the distance, among the tips of the dark green fir trees, the clear blue cupolas of a small village church. A lump comes to your throat, your heart overflows with a mysterious feeling of oneness with the forest, the river, and the church whose cross shines so brilliantly in the sunshine.

These, at any rate, were the thoughts that passed through my head on that day, 25 April 1986, as I walked through the woods with my family. It was springtime. A sense of freedom and renewal was in the air. The trembling blue petals of the crocuses were pushing up through last year's withered leaves. My two-year-old son, Sasha, knelt down by each flower to contemplate it.

We did not know—no-one yet knew—that a few hours later something would happen which would transform for ever this ancient wonderland, this forest, these fields and meadows, our whole lives. And that from now on, life on earth would not only be divided into epochs and eras, civilisations, religions and political systems, but also into 'before' and 'after' Chernobyl. The earth would never be the same as it had been before 26 April 1986 at twenty-four minutes past one . . .

Zhitomir is 130 km from Kiev, the capital of the Ukraine. My husband and I sometimes spend an evening at the theatre there. We generally come straight home after the show, arriving back between midnight and one o'clock.

By a twist of fate, on 27 April, suspecting nothing—neither the radio, the television, nor the newspapers had mentioned the explosion which had happened at the Chernobyl nuclear reactor—we went to Kiev. The Japanese group 'Setiku' were performing that evening at the Ukrainian Palace of Culture. We left our car in an adjoining parking lot. I remember that the show was something quite special. It was great art: I can still see the all-white costumes of the players, the grace of their movements.

We left late in the evening, in an excellent mood. The road from Kiev to Zhitomir was drowned in the blossoming spring forests. Halfway home, we stopped and got out of the car to breathe the intoxicating greenness. Everything was silent. Cold stars glittered. On one side we could see quite clearly the Great Bear, like a ladle. The moon lit up everything clearly. We could almost hear the buds bursting on the trees next to us.

Rumours Spread

Although no official information about the Chernobyl reactor had been provided by the official Soviet media, in the neighbouring towns of Kiev, Zhitomir and Chernigov panic grew daily. No-one knew exactly what had happened, and the rumours were getting wilder and wilder. Iodine disappeared from chemists' shops. Many people thought that it could protect you from radiation, and they drank it neat, burning their throats and digestive tracts. The official medical services were silent. Eventually, after ten days, the Ukrainian Minister of Health, A. Romanyenko, gave us this precious advice: shut your windows and wipe your shoes carefully with a damp rag before entering a house. Wipe floors and furniture with a damp duster. These were all the precautions we were to take against the radioactivity.

It was from foreign radio broadcasts that we learnt that Block number 4 of the Chernobyl power station had blown up and that the radiation level had risen. Our official media only made the announcement two days later.

The joyful May Day festival was approaching and nobody would have believed that something terrible and ineradicable had happened. On 1 May, at Zhitomir, Kiev, Chernigov, in all the towns and villages of Ukraine, Byelorussia, Russia, the Baltic lands, all over the country, as in previous years, millions of people lined the streets. It was extremely hot. Not just mild, but hot. Children dressed in national costume, breathing radioactive fumes, danced on the Kreshchatik, the main street of the Ukrainian capital. On the stand, greeting the crowds, stood the members of the Ukrainian Politburo, government ministers, and invited guests. At almost precisely the same moment, senior civil servants were hurrying their children to Borispol airport to get them away from the scene of the catastrophe. The children of the betrayed workers and intellectuals were left behind to delight the eyes of the ministers; this was the price paid to give international opinion the illusion that all was well.

My friend Nina Smykovskaya, a journalist whom I had known since university days, and whom God had at last blessed with children at the age of forty, was not able to leave for her family home in Odessa until 7 May. By then panic had swept through Kiev. Nina went into labour early, at seven months, and gave birth to twins. She named them after the women who helped her in those terrible hours, Diana and Inna. The babies were weak and anaemic; their mother, not suspecting any danger, fed them for two weeks on milk which was full of iodine and radioactive caesium. When they were two months old, the doctors ordered an emergency total blood transfusion. The children were saved, but to this day one of them, Diana, has developed more slowly than the other. Nina explained to me that one had been injected with fresh blood, and the other with older, preserved blood. Now when they celebrate their birthday, it is the anniversary of the tragedy. Their life is difficult: their parents, both journalists, only have a tiny apartment. When I stay the night with them in Kiev, Victor has to sleep in the tiny kitchen while I have his bed-settee.

Escape

I remember very well the beginning of May that fateful year. A blue sky. Snowy white clouds. Heat. It was strange. Rumours were all around us. After the first of May they began to snowball.

The radio and newspapers told us one thing, then people coming from the worst hit areas told us another. All seats on trains and planes leaving Kiev were booked up for months ahead. People were at their wit's end, terrified by the unknown, and were storming the trains. They wanted to go away, anywhere, as far as possible from Chernobyl.

I was no exception. My husband Alexander is a fireman, and some of his colleagues had been sent to Chernobyl to pump water under the destroyed reactor. On 7 May he telephoned me from work to try and persuade me to leave with the children. Easy to say—but where could we go? At that time I was working on the 'Industry and construction' column of the local Party newspaper *Radianska Zhitomirshchina.*

I put in a request for leave with the editor-in-chief. My section head made it a condition that before I went, I finished a paper on the construction of a factory at Krochna. The next morning the paper was on his desk. It began with a sentence about the blossoming flowers around Zhitomir, and the wonderful scent of apples which wafted over the factory from the neighbouring gardens . . .

We were not able to get seats on the flight to Armavir, a small town in the northern Caucasus where we had relatives. There were no more tickets to be had, not to Armavir, nor to any other destination. We only just managed to get seats on a train to Moscow, to stay with friends.

The scene at Zhitomir station resembled an Exodus. My eldest son, Milan, who was then in the fifth grade [Year 7], was unable to complete his last term at school. All parents who were able had been given permission to take their children out of school before the end of the school year.

The whole family came to the station: my mother, my husband's parents, my sister. We all held back our tears. The grandmothers joked with little Sasha and gave him cakes, sweets, apples, toys. I was showered with advice and Milan, the eldest, was made to promise to be good and help me during the journey. It is eighteen hours by train from Zhitomir to Moscow. It was my youngest son's second birthday. We spent it on the train, surrounded by people just like ourselves, exhausted, overcome by misfortune.

We had no family in Moscow and I had rarely had any reason to go there. I had been once when I was in my third year at university, and a second time for work to report on the Exhibition of

Achievements of the National Economy. The first time, I had seen nothing of the town, because I was thinking about a man I was in love with who was not there. The second time, Moscow had won my heart with its churches and little streets with pretty old names. For me, this is what makes all the charm of the capital.

This time, we were in no mood for sightseeing. We were met at the station by some Jewish friends of ours, Fayina Alexandrovna and her son Misha, who had used to live in Zhitomir, and who still spent their holidays there as they had inherited a house in the district. Misha was a student.

When we arrived at their house, the first thing we did was to take off all our clothes and wash them straight away. I did not know what level of radioactivity they might contain, but I was instinctively aware of danger.

I am grateful to these people who took us in, as I know that some people who had fled from the radiation found themselves ostracised in the places they fled to; other people thought them contagious.

We stayed with these friends for several days. They lived in a small flat in one of those poor-quality houses built in a hurry in the [Nikita] Khrushchev era, and I could see that we were in the way. I managed to get tickets to Armavir. My cousins were waiting for us there, and we arrived on 14 May after an exhausting, twenty-four hour journey by train from Moscow-Adler.

The weather there was already hot. The first cherries were being picked. The garden was fragrant. Everything was calm, no-one talked much about Chernobyl; it was as if they were not affected. (Three years later, I was to learn that the area of Krasnodar had also been contaminated by radiation.)

The first thing I did was to take the children to the local radiological station. The level of radioactivity on their clothes was normal for the region: 0.025 milliroentgens. At home, before Chernobyl, it was 0.017. They explained that the difference was due to the nearby Caucasus.

Despite the flowers and the heat, we did not find peace in Armavir. My youngest son fell ill. We saw a local doctor, a woman, who was all the more attentive when she learned that we came from the Ukraine. That might not seem extraordinary, but knowing Soviet medicine, we were especially grateful. Sasha was suffering from a sore throat and bronchitis together.

By the time he was better, my leave was up, and in June we

had to go back to Zhitomir. The news from there was more or less reassuring. I could not leave the children in the Caucasus, there was no-one to look after them. I had to go back to work—I could not leave it—a Soviet family cannot live on just one salary.

A torrid summer awaited us. *Pravda* administered daily tranquillisers by the million in the form of soothing articles. I am still ashamed of the titles of some of my colleagues' articles: 'The song of the nightingales above Pripyat', 'Small mementos of the reactor', etc. These 'mementos' cost the health of millions of people in the region. . . .

It seems to me that all through the summer of 1986, not one drop of rain fell on the town. The sky was a uniform pale blue, faded by the pitiless sun. The reactor had at last been sealed, after an incredible amount of sand, lead and other materials had been poured into it. Its 'funeral' was celebrated. Relatives wept over the lead coffins of the victims of the radiation. The engineers from the power station were sentenced. Was it all over? No, it had only just started. It was only three or four years after the catastrophe that we began to realise its extent, its fatal nature and to perceive the truth about our sick society. The bell is tolling. Will we be able to hear it in the primitive depths of our communist cavern, deafened as we are by the ideology of self-satisfaction?

The Palestinian *Intifada* Begins:
December 8, 1987

Palestinian Riots Erupt into a Major Uprising

by Ze'ev Schiff and Ehud Ya'ari

In December 1987 a seemingly ordinary traffic accident galvanized
Palestinian communities living in the Israeli-occupied territories
and started what would become a bitter six-year uprising against Israeli authority. Tensions had been simmering in Arab settlements
since 1967, when Israel's victory over a coalition of Arab forces left
it in possession of Arab lands. Life in the Arab settlements of the
occupied territories was not easy. Many Arabs lived in overcrowded
and squalid conditions in poverty-stricken towns like Jebalya. For
twenty years, anger, desperation, and resentment had been building
in these settlements, and on December 8, 1987, when an Israeli
truck hit a car carrying Arab workers and killed four of the passengers, the fuse was lit.

News of the accident spread quickly. By the afternoon, Palestinians all across the occupied territories erupted into mass demonstrations and riots. Rock- and bottle-throwing mobs harassed Israeli
soldiers and stormed police barracks. Arab students and workers
went on strike, and isolated police squads soon found themselves
running for their lives. Officials, both Israeli and those of the Palestinian Liberation Organization (PLO), were shocked at how the rioting became so widespread in such a short time. The Israeli government and the PLO were both equally unprepared to deal with the
uprising.

Ze'ev Schiff and Ehud Ya'ari, *Intifada*, edited and translated by Ina Friedman. New York:
Touchstone, 1989. Copyright © 1989 by Domino Press. English Translation Copyright 1990
by Ina Friedman. Reproduced by permission of Simon & Schuster Macmillan.

According to Israeli reporters and authors Ze'ev Schiff and Ehud Ya'ari, the Israeli government and the PLO looked at the uprising, which became known as the *Intifada*, in a purely political manner. In the following essay Schiff and Ya'ari contend that although the *Intifada* was to have far-reaching political consequences, its roots were economic. The Palestinians who started the uprising were protesting against rampant unemployment and the sheer lack of prospects and opportunities for Arabs of the occupied territories. The PLO later put a political spin on the uprising and parlayed it into a call for autonomy in the occupied territories.

The PLO's strategy eventually yielded results. In 1993, the sixth year of the *Intifada*, PLO chief Yasser Arafat and Israeli prime minister Yitzhak Rabin signed the Oslo Accords in Norway. In the agreement, Rabin granted the Palestinians limited autonomy. He also recognized the PLO as the legitimate Palestinian authority, promised to curtail Jewish settlement of Arab lands, and agreed to withdraw Israeli troops from Arab settlements. It was an incredibly unpopular move for Rabin. Many Israelis felt he was giving up too much, and Rabin came to be seen as a traitor to the Jewish people. Many experts believe that Rabin's assassination at the hands of a right-wing Jewish militant in 1995 was a direct result of his endorsement of the Oslo Accords.

Though winter had already set in by then, the evening of Tuesday, December 8, 1987, was a warm one in Gaza, and the air was particularly close in Jebalya, the largest refugee camp in the [Gaza] Strip. The heaviness permeating the air that night was a detail that would long be remembered by the Israeli soldiers manning the outpost in the camp, for December 8 was the evening on which the Palestinian uprising broke out. In a sense, it was fitting that the explosion should occur in Jebalya, where some 60,000 people make their home in conditions of appalling poverty, overcrowding, and filth. The violence on December 8 was directed specifically against the army outpost and the soldiers holding it—a company of reservists under the command of a computer programmer and a moshavnik from the Negev [a hilly desert region in southern Israel]. They were the first to experience the surprise that hit the entire Israeli army, indeed all of Israel. But unlike most others, they were to bear the brunt of it—and in more ways than one.

For all intents and purposes, December 8 had been a day like most others in the Gaza Strip. Admittedly, a fatal traffic accident had occurred there in the afternoon, but traffic deaths are so commonplace in Israel and the territories that it often seems the public is totally inured to them. In this case an Israeli truck had hit a car carrying laborers from the Gaza Strip, immediately killing four of the passengers and badly injuring the others. The item was broadcast over the radio as a matter of course—another statistic that was expected to faze almost no one. Then something odd happened: all at once, it seemed, Gaza was abuzz with a wild rumor that was to spark off an unprecedented wave of demonstrations. The crash, this rumor had it, had not been an accident at all but a cold-blooded act of vengeance by a relative of the Israeli stabbed to death in Gaza's main market two days earlier. And by the same token that the crash was no accident, to the residents of both the Gaza Strip and the West Bank the rumor was no rumor but an indisputable fact. By evening a leaflet was already in circulation in Gaza denouncing the killing of the four Palestinians, and the following day the Arabic newspaper *al-Fajr*, published in East Jerusalem, pronounced the death of the four passengers to have been "maliciously perpetrated." Even the mayor of Nablus, Hafez Toukan—an Israeli appointee—took the trouble to protest the "murder" of the four innocent men and declared a day of mourning in his city.

The Rioting Spreads

As soon as news of the fatal accident had been broadcast on the radio, the officers of the company in Jebalya sensed that there would be trouble when the funerals took place. But their concern was not shared by all. The head of the army's Southern Command, Maj. Gen. Yitzhak (Itzik) Mordechai, was not even informed of the accident; one of his men evidently decided that since no military personnel were involved, there was no point in "bothering" the general with the news. The men in Jebalya were right to feel uneasy, though. As thousands of mourners returned from the funerals early in the evening, their procession turned into an outright assault on the outpost. Crowds of angry people, young and old, closed in on the barbed-wire fence and began throwing stones into the compound. Shots fired in the air did nothing to deter the rioters, who were shouting curses and chanting the cry *"Jihad! Jihad!"* A patrol was sent out to disperse the demonstrators, but they only regrouped and surrounded the outpost again. Soon rioting had spread throughout the camp, as other army and Border Police patrols became the targets of stones and firebombs. In the past, demonstrations and other disturbances had always broken up at nightfall, when the residents closed themselves up in their homes. This time the rioting began at dusk and continued well past eleven o'clock.

Tired and shaken by the force of the outburst, a few of the reserve company's officers met at the entrance to the Jebalya outpost before turning in for the night. When one of them commented that unless the army sent a conspicuous infusion of reinforcements into the camp there would be trouble the next day as well, the sector commander could hardly contain his impatience. "Nothing's going to happen!" he scoffed at the reservists so easily rattled by the violence. "You don't know these people. They'll go to sleep now and leave for work first thing in the morning, as usual. You'll see."

No additional forces were sent to Gaza. Neither was Jebalya placed under curfew. But few people slept in the camp that night, and by dawn most of its roads and alleyways had been blocked by a combination of heavy rocks, broken furniture, and steel pipes (brought in to repair the chronically insufficient sewage system). One of the army's night patrols saw what was happening but received orders to wait until dawn before dealing with the problem. Meanwhile, the reserve company's fifty-five men closed themselves up in the outpost and waited for the inevitable.

The Next Day Starts Badly

Contrary to the sector commander's confident prediction, the next day boded ill from the very start. Most of Jebalya's residents did not go to work, and by six A.M. the rioting had already flared up again. Students of the Islamic University were milling around the streets of Gaza city, calling on people to come out and demonstrate. In nearby Jebalya thousands of people already filled the streets and countless others stood on their roofs waiting expectantly. A pall of rage hovered over the camp, and there was little reason to doubt that the appearance of troops would trigger an explosion. Nevertheless, out of the compound came two armored personnel carriers (APCs) preceded by a jeep. Their aim was to break through the roadblocks and make a show of strength, but their mission was doomed from the start. As they moved along the narrow axis dividing the two quarters of the camp, thousands of people stood lining the road and at the windows of their huts and houses, practically touching the vehicles as they passed. At first the soldiers were met by jeers and curses, but soon stones began flying and the men in the APCs realized that if they didn't close the flaps they would be knocked out by the missiles coming from every direction, including the rooftops. A Molotov cocktail hurled out of one of the buildings missed its mark but burst into flames on the street, filling the air with the pungent odor of gasoline. A few daring young Palestinians actually jumped onto the APCs, forcing their drivers to floor the gas pedal and deliberately swerve their vehicles from side to side in an attempt to shake them off.

On one of these zigzags a machine gun and its tripod fell off an APC, and a number of people rushed forward to snatch it. It took a burst of gunfire, while the vehicle was traveling in reverse, to stop them from getting to the weapon, but two of the Palestinians did manage to run off with the ammunition belt. The rioters were not daunted by the shots fired in the air. On the contrary, again and again the soldiers were confronted by frenzied people taunting them in Hebrew and daring them to shoot while they stood rooted to the spot in defiance. Others let out cries of despair—"It's better to die than to go on like this!"—as though the reservists had the power to change their fate or the abominable conditions in the camp. Soon it was evident that the APCs were quite useless in that situation—especially as standing orders forbade the men to fire indiscriminately into a crowd—and the patrol was ordered to return to the outpost. . . .

The Warning Signs

For those willing to see them, there had been countless signs that serious trouble was afoot in the territories, and certainly the uprising did not break out abruptly after a period of calm. In the course of 1987, and especially during the latter half of the year, various symptoms made themselves so manifest that either all of Israel had gone blind or those who did make out the drift of events simply chose to ignore it. The boldness of the demonstrators in the territories had reached the point where they were attempting to attack Israeli soldiers, including high-ranking officers, and snatch their weapons away. In August an Israeli officer was shot and killed at midday on the main street of Gaza before the eyes of dozens of people—none of whom made an effort to help him or even called for an ambulance. Firing into the air to disperse demonstrations had become a fruitless exercise; the demonstrators merely jeered at the troops, as though intent on drawing them into a confrontation. More than once in the course of November, Israeli employees of the Civil Administration abandoned their cars in panic on the streets of Gaza, later to find only their charred remains. Many of the actions that were to characterize the uprising—throwing stones and firebombs at Israeli vehicles and during demonstrations, distributing leaflets on how to operate against Israel, holding commercial and school strikes, and showing the Palestinian flag—had actually been current during the months before its outbreak. A perusal of the operations log kept by the Civil Administration in Gaza showed a steep rise in most kinds of civil disturbances over the previous year: 133 percent in the number of demonstrations and riots, 178 percent in the burning of tires (487 incidents up from 172), 140 percent in the throwing of stones, and 68 percent in the blocking of roads.

The more these incidents multiplied, the more difficult it was for the Israel Defense Force (IDF) to bring them to a halt, and the more Israel appeared weak in Palestinian eyes. With the army's deterrent image badly battered, the Palestinians had less to fear from Israel's clout, and their boldness began to escalate. After the murder of the IDF officer in Gaza, the employees of the Civil Administration were ordered to commute to their jobs in groups, so that many of them traveled in convoys—and even then they shunned the main road through Gaza, preferring a circuitous route that bypasses most of the Strip. There was nothing secret about this new arrangement; it functioned day in and day out in full view of the Gazans, who made a habit of standing outside the administration's headquarters to watch the stream of Israeli vehicles pass through the gates. Moreover, most of the Civil Administration's staff, including its complement of army officers, made a point of leaving Gaza before dark. Some Israelis actually preferred, whenever possible, to use cars with Gazan license plates. In time even the military was given orders to skirt the obstacles laid on the roads and avoid clashing with rioters. None of this was lost on the Palestinians, of course. A survey conducted by the Civil Administration showed that the local population took these precautions to be a sign of cowardice and concluded that "the rioters have placed the Israeli administration under siege." As the investigating officer would ultimately phrase it: "The erosion in our image did not occur overnight; it was a process of retreat, concession, and hesitation, a collection of small victories over the administration, with each little triumph having reverberations ten times greater than the actual significance of the victory itself."

Caught Off Guard

Yet despite this protracted buildup of confidence, when the periodic incidents turned into a bona fide uprising that spread to the West Bank as well, Israel was surprised—and not just on the tactical level, as certain government and military figures would now have us believe. Until the uprising the Israelis knew that they must be prepared to fight on two fronts: a regular war against standing armies and both an open and secret war against terrorism. By their rebellion, however, the Palestinians opened a third front of mass, unarmed, civilian violence—a new kind of warfare for which Israel had no effective response. Since the standard tools of military might are not designed to handle defiance of this sort, the IDF was wholly unprepared for the uprising in terms of its deployment, its combat doctrine, and even its store of the most basic equipment. The result was that overnight Israel was exposed in all its weakness, which was perhaps the real import of the surprise. The shock of being caught off guard was further aggravated by Israel's failure in addressing world public opinion; it was simply incapable of making a case for its position while its army was shooting down unarmed women and children.

Much of the surprise was about the way in which the Palestinians conducted themselves. The Military Government had been dealing with sporadic outbreaks of rioting for years, but they had usually been the work of students and other young people guided by the Palestinian organizations. This time the outburst was spontaneous and encompassed the entire population: young and old, male and female, town and country, religious and secular. But above all it was the sheer number of people that catapulted the riots into a full-blown uprising. The revolt spread like wildfire to cities, villages, and refugee camps. None was prepared to oppose it; indeed, the sense of solidarity during the first months of the uprising had never been stronger in Palestinian society, long known for its divisiveness. Israel was no less astonished by the readiness of the Palestinians to bear the weight of casualties and suffering, from over 500 dead and 8,500 wounded in the first two years of the insurgency to long commercial strikes, weeks without working or bringing in pay, and oppressive curfews and blockades. Equally unexpected was their self-restraint. Despite their animosity and rage, the Palestinians did not resort to arms—giving them a distinct advantage in the contest for sympathetic public opinion. There was a modest collection of arms within the territories, and even these few weapons could have wreaked havoc among unsuspecting Israelis, especially civilians. But the Palestinians appreciated almost instinctively that restraint was in their own self-interest; resort to arms would only justify the IDF's sweeping use of its far superior fire power and cause the Palestinians punishing losses. . . .

No One Assumed Responsibility

That the gathering storm went unnoticed can probably be traced to the fact that no single person or agency regarded itself as fully responsible for the territories, so that from an administrative standpoint the subject was allowed to fall between all the possible stools. Neither did any one officer or official believe himself responsible for assessing what was likely to happen there or for gauging the perils that Israel would face by continuing to control a million and a half Palestinians who did not want to be subject to its rule. Various bodies within the defense establishment each focused its attention on a specific aspect of the broad subject of "the territories," yet neither the prime minister nor the minister of defense—who should have been aware of the gaps—called for a change in the structure of the system. The same held for the Ministerial Committee for Security Affairs, which had a number of former defense ministers among its members. . . .

At various times Labor ministers appointed ad hoc groups of experts to advise them on the territories. Shimon Peres had a team that included the Arabist Emanuel Sivan. Gad Ya'akobi, the minister of economy and planning, put together a group that included, in addition to Sivan, the former military commander of the West Bank, Benyamin Ben-Eliezer, and ex-intelligence chief Shlomo Gazit. At a meeting held early in 1986, the consensus among these men was that the creation of a clear policy on the territories was long overdue. Ben-Eliezer even warned that a rebellion was in the offing if the political and economic problems in the territories continued to go untended. Yet these frameworks, if not perfunctory, were highly limited in their influence both because their findings were not circulated through the standard channels and because no minister ever made a crusade out of the information gleaned from his experts.

And a crusade was what it would have taken to make the country sit up and listen. For the sad truth is that when it came to the occupied territories and their Palestinian inhabitants, there seemed to be a collective mental block in Israel that the national leadership, most of the experts, and even a large portion of the press was unable to overcome. The Jewish public tended to repress the Palestinian issue entirely, relating to the territories as though they were a distant land. In a sense the Israelis discovered the territories twice: at the end of the Six-Day War, when attention was riveted on their historical landscape with all its biblical landmarks, and again some twenty years later, in December 1987, when the Palestinian population made it impossible for them to cling to the blinders that had made the million and a half Arabs under Israeli military rule so conveniently invisible. In the interim, however, a new conception had taken hold: that the Palestinians were not a factor in the Middle East equation. Above all, this conclusion was reached because the Palestinians simply did not exist in the political consciousness of most Israelis. Yet it was supposedly justified by the reasoning that since they had no aspirations other than the destruction of the State of Israel, the Palestinians had disqualified themselves as partners to negotiations on the settlement of the Middle East conflict. Both the major parties in Israel, Labor and the Likud, were at most prepared to accord the Palestinians oblique recognition by discussing their problem with others— the Jordanians, the Egyptians, or the Americans—but never with the Palestinians themselves. Curiously enough, the Arabs had once taken a similar tack by obliterating the word Israel from all their books and maps, insisting that there was no such place and that any negotiations on the Middle East dispute would have to be conducted through the United States. Israel's adoption of a parallel policy toward the Palestinians had a similarly damping effect on the peace process.

The block of the two major parties was evident in every step they took. As far as the Israeli Right was and is concerned, the territories might as well be a virgin wilderness, as the Arabs inhabiting them are regarded as little more than tree trunks. The conclusions that beg to be drawn from the demographic patterns of the two peoples living in the Greater Land of Israel are irrelevant to right-wingers; otherwise they would concede that if the territories are incorporated into Israel, the Jews will soon become a minority in their own state! Those members of the Right who do apprehend the dangers inherent in their plan to annex the territories have begun to espouse a so-called transfer of their Arab inhabitants. But despite all efforts to befog the issue and even portray it as a humanitarian gesture, since it is unimaginable that the Palestinians would leave their homes of their own accord, the real import of their proposed "transfer" is expulsion. . . .

Intifada

"Uprising" does not begin to do justice to the Arabic word *intifada*, which soon became the rubric for the explosion in the occupied territories. Its literal meaning is the shivering that grips a person suffering from fever, or the persistent shaking of a dog infested with fleas; but in political terms it has always been associated with relatively limited or brief upheavals, such as the Kurdish revolt, the 1983 split within the Fatah, and even the 1977 riots in Cairo. The "copyright" on its use in the Israeli-Palestinian context belongs to Yasser Arafat, who failed to see in the early reports reaching his desk anything out of the ordinary about the eruption of riots in the territories. Since he regarded the events in Gaza as just another spasm of violence that would pass within days, it did not occur to him to offer a more appropriate name for the phenomenon—or, in fact, to treat the situation any differently than he had similar instances in the past. (Shortly before his death in April 1988, Arafat's deputy, Halil al-Wazir—better known as Abu Jihad—coined another term for the events in the territories: "*haba*," meaning storm or tempest. But by that point "*intifada*" had already stuck.) So it was that the "sole legitimate representative" of the Palestinians living under occupation displayed much the same blindness as the occupiers. . . .

The *intifada* was an assertion of defiance that bubbled up from below, a statement by the legions of Palestinian youth who felt bereft of a future; the high school and university students doomed to choose between indignity and exile; the tens of thousands of laborers who made their living in Israel but were expected to remain invisible; the veterans of Israeli prisons who were more convinced than ever of the justice of their cause but saw their people sinking deeper and deeper into hopelessness. In short, it was the work of the Palestinian masses, and that is why it surprised everyone: the complacent Israeli authorities, the over-confident Jordanians, the self-satisfied Palestinian Liberation Organization (PLO) leadership, and even local Palestinians regarded as influential figures in the territories. A popular revolt with all the hallmarks of a genuine revolution, it erupted suddenly and created a new strategy for the Palestinian struggle that confounded both the PLO establishment, scrambling wildly to keep up with events from afar, and the native leadership whose constituents were suddenly spinning out of control. Above all, however, it delivered a sharp reminder to the Israelis that they simply could not go on blithely ignoring the twenty-year-old Palestinian problem festering right in the middle of their collective lap.

The Tiananmen Square Massacre and Its Impact on China

by the *Economist*

In April 1989 Chinese students began to gather in Beijing's Tiananmen Square to pay tribute to recently deceased Communist Party reformer Hu Yaobang, a prominent advocate of China's political and economic liberalization. Hu Yaobang had been purged from the government by a hard-line Communist faction, which was led by Deng Xiaoping and Li Peng, because he did not harshly crack down on student demonstrations in 1987. Though the gathering in Tiananmen had started as a tribute to Hu Yaobang, it quickly evolved into a protest against the hard-liners and rampant corruption within the Communist Party. By the end of May, the gathering of students had swelled into a crowd of more than one hundred thousand protesters, and more were joining the demonstrations every day. When the government attempted to send troops into the square to clear it, many Beijing residents barricaded the streets and blocked their advance.

The crowd of protesters in Tiananmen exacerbated the split that had been forming in the Chinese government between reform-minded politicians like Hu Yaobang and Communist Party chief Zhao Ziyang and hard-liners like Deng Xiaoping. Wishing a peaceful end to the protest, Zhao Ziyang had been making conciliatory gestures toward the students in Tiananmen, promising to heed reasonable requests through democratic means. The hard-liners, however, mindful of the wave of reform that had begun to sweep through the crumbling Communist governments of Eastern Europe, had no intention of giving in to student demands. Zhao Ziyang was removed from his post and placed under house arrest, along with a number of other reformers, and the troops that had been surrounding Tiananmen Square—many of whom started to show sympathy for the protesters—were replaced by troops loyal to the hard-liners. In the early morning of June 4, 1989, they opened fire.

The crackdown on the demonstration illustrated the limit of the reforms the Chinese government wished to pursue. Though it was eager to modernize the economy and play a bigger part in world trade, political freedom was something the Chinese government was not yet ready to grant. The crisis allowed the hard-line faction of the Chinese government to solidify its hold on power and purge the leadership of those who advocated political freedom.

In the following excerpt, the editors of the *Economist*, a British journal of news and opinion, examine the state of China ten years after the Tiananmen Square massacre. The editors contend that the aftershocks of the 1989 crackdown continue to be felt in China, as victims demand an accounting of the dead and an official apology. The government, however, continues to insist that its response to the protesters was appropriate and refuses to acknowledge any wrongdoing. In the meantime, China has instituted dramatic economic reforms and has substantially decentralized its government. In addition, China is showing signs of democratic reform, especially in the rural areas.

Since the bloody crackdown on June 4th 1989, China and its government have changed hugely for the better. But only when the country has dealt honestly with its past can it squarely face the future.

A decade ago [1989], China was seething with discontent. In many cities students and workers had joined forces to protest at Communist Party corruption, and at the lack of accountability and democracy that allowed it to flourish unchecked. Now, frustration is again rising in China, but this time the anger is being turned on China's foreign critics, not its own failings.

Indeed, many thoughtful Chinese worry that mounting foreign criticism of China plays into the hands of Communist hardliners [those most likely to limit personal freedoms] opposed to any kind of political reform. Frustration is turning to despair as relations with America plummet in the wake of NATO's [May 7, 1999] bombing of China's embassy in Belgrade, China's abrupt suspension of negotiations to gain entry to the World Trade Organisation (WTO), the publication of the Cox report on China's scooping up of America's weapons secrets and, most recently, a congressional resolution condemning the Tiananmen crackdown a decade ago. "Look," says one who fell foul of the authorities back then, "Tiananmen is behind us."

Effects of Crackdown Linger

Not so for some of the families who were killed when troops crushed the protest. [In June 1999] the relatives of 105 of the victims took the unprecedented action of turning to the courts in support of their demand for a criminal investigation.

Among the relatives is Ding Zilin, a retired philosophy professor at Beijing University, who had kept her head firmly in her books until the day, ten years ago, when her 17-year-old son was shot dead. She has since spent her time contacting the relatives of others who died during the Tiananmen crackdown, counting the victims, and demanding an explanation, an apology and compensation from the Communist Party. This is how she describes her life now:

Since May 4th my husband and I have been blocked from leaving campus. We can walk around campus, and we can shop at the little store on the grounds, but we can't leave. How do I feel? Well, my husband and I say that this is "house arrest with Chinese characteristics". There are a dozen or more young men outside my house who say that if I try to leave campus they will take me away. This is like invisible violence.

The Chinese government, in other words, has not been able to put Tiananmen behind it either. The protests, officially, were deemed a "counter-revolutionary rebellion". Government leaders still insist that this was the "correct" verdict and that it will never be changed. One day presumably it will be. But for now, the events of 1989, when the Communist Party leadership visibly lost its grip and very nearly fell from power, are not up for public discussion. The year is a blank sheet in the official history.

The party general secretary who fell from grace that year, Zhao Ziyang, sits under house arrest, allowed out for the occasional game of golf.

Reevaluating the Crackdown

Time appears to be on the government's side. Many Chinese shudder at Russia's recent political and economic chaos. Where students a decade ago chanted "Give us a Gorbachev", most people today say "Thank God for Deng Xiaoping". This change was apparent in the public reaction to the NATO embassy bombing. The Tiananmen students thought they were saving a nation whose political decay seemed to put it at risk of being carved up by foreigners, as had happened in the past. On posters Deng Xiaoping was caricatured as the 19th-century empress dowager, Cixi. Last month [May 1999], by contrast, calls to maintain social stability seemed to resonate as deeply with today's students as did the government's fiercely nationalistic tone. After three days, the demonstrations outside America's embassy ended obediently.

As the "unofficial" verdict on Tiananmen has subtly changed over time, the government might be said to have won its propaganda campaign to depict the peaceful protests as something more. Whatever revulsion there was at the crackdown, without it, many people now say, China could not have marshalled the will to throw itself into a full-blown modernisation of the economy. Even some of those who wish democracy for China now regret the 1989 events. Their result, says one economist, was to set back democratic prospects for years.

China Prior to Tiananmen

To gauge just what has changed in China in the 1990s, it is worth recalling the state of the country on the eve of the protests. After ten years of "reform and opening up", China's leaders seemed to have lost the agenda. Inflation was rising, and goods of every kind were hard to find. . . . The party ruled with a casual tyranny, corrupt and nepotistic.

Frustration was perhaps highest among intellectuals, a point distilled in *Evening Chats in Beijing,* a book of conversations with Chinese intellectuals on the eve of the protests, written by a Princeton professor, Perry Link:

By 1988 . . . the questions intellectuals were raising did not have any ready answers—or any answers at all. . . . Why were we intellectuals so docile in the 1950s when Mao "criticised" us and set up his tyranny? What do we make of the "peasant consciousness" that we admired then but that oppresses us now? How can we feel certain that we have really understood the Cultural Revolution? Given the absurdity of blaming [that] on just a "gang" of only four people, what is it in all of us that allowed such violence to happen?

The questioning came at a time when economic reforms had run up against the Leninist constraints of a social system that tied each person to his work-unit and that made even the most mundane activity—getting a telephone installed, buying a hotplate, getting permission for research—a nightmarish obstacle course of petty bribes and fawning to superiors. What happened next was played out on television screens around the world (and even, for a while, in China), culminating in bloodshed as the popular mutiny, after much dithering, was put down with appalling severity.

Evening chats in Beijing these days often revolve around a series of what ifs. What if the Chinese leadership had swept Tiananmen Square of students sooner? Or had established a dialogue sooner? What if the authorities had owned a few water-cannon and known about crowd control? Surely the army would then not have been ordered to fire on its own people. Once it had done so, at Deng Xiaoping's orders, the Communist Party imposed a new contract on the country: hard-fisted political control in return for a fast pace of economic modernisation.

Economic and Political Change

The economic consequences are hard to exaggerate, for they represent, in many sectors, the wholesale retreat of the state. Some $200 billion of foreign investment has come to China in the past decade, and foreign-funded ventures account for over half of China's exports. The private sector now accounts for perhaps one third of the economy, up from almost nothing, and some state companies have started to act like private ones. If goods were hard to come by in 1989, today there are too many of them: consumers are spoilt for choice. Some 1.5m new fixed telephone lines are laid each month, and China will soon be the second-biggest mobile-phone market in the world. Graduates in the 1980s were told where to work. Today they dive into a competitive market. Private housing, unheard of a decade ago, is catching on. Mechanisms of state control—the household-registration system, the work-unit system, the one-child policy—have been greatly weakened. Talk in China is free, so long as it is not deemed openly to challenge the state. The new prosperity is still too unevenly spread. And wrenching change has brought the uncertainties of unemployment to many. But the greatest number of Chinese are beneficiaries, not victims.

But can the political system keep up with these changes, and adapt itself without violence? The Communist Party has cleaned house. More room has been made in government for younger, more meritocratic types—including June 4th protesters. The National People's Congress (NPC) takes its job of monitoring the government's performance seriously. It has also become a main centre for drafting laws, calling upon foreign legal experts for help. Under the hand of Zhu Rongji, the prime minister, central government has shrunk. A reorganisation of the central bank along regional lines is a big step towards improving economic management. A measure of competency, in other words, is spreading through the system.

One of the biggest changes has come at the grassroots, where "village" democracy is now practised by the two-thirds of Chinese living in rural areas. At the top, power is no longer wielded by individuals with the stature of Mao Zedong or Deng Xiaoping, who died in 1997. Today's Politburo leaders, under the president, Jiang Zemin, need to look elsewhere for their authority. The party is fast learning the techniques of focus groups, opinion polls and complaint hotlines. Communists can learn to kiss babies, too.

Change should not be exaggerated. Power wielded at the top is still of an intensely personal kind. The inscrutable senior leadership helps give an air of stability. But there are still no mechanisms for the smooth exercise of power, or for its transfer. Lacking transparency, much of government is still choked by incompetence and corruption.

The party has bolstered its legitimacy since Tiananmen, yet that does not mean people do not want political change. Where might it come from? The democratic movement is widely written off. Its most articulate proponents—such as Fang Lizhi, Liu Binyan and Wei Jingsheng—are in exile. One exiled Tiananmen hero, Wang Dan, has come in for vituperative abuse on the Beijing University campus where he was once a hero, for daring to suggest that the embassy bombing in Belgrade might have been a genuine mistake.

Yet those who claim that real dissent has been snuffed out may underestimate the adaptability of the new democratic opposition, spearheaded by the Chinese Democracy Party. Though two of its leaders were given stiff jail sentences last December [1998] and a score or so members have been detained in a pre-Tiananmen round-up, the party is probably much bigger than most people think—with several thousand active members around the country, drawn from all walks of life.

Besides, democracy activists have changed their tactics, if not their goals. Many seem to want to put the idea of revolution, which has driven most political change this century in China, behind them. Democrats now seek a more subtle, long-term game of participation. As one leader of the Chinese Democracy Party, Ren Wanding, argues, political change should not be pushed too far: "Just one step at a time. That way, we can nurture our democratic forces as well as give the government time to change. That's good for both sides."

Perhaps most intriguing is the contention by some in government that change could come swiftly, as village democracy spreads from the countryside into the cities. Once that happens, it will be hard to prevent competitive politics from taking over.

For now, though, it is hard for urbanites to grasp why swathes of the countryside have taken to elections for village leaders with such gusto. Wang Zhenyao, a senior official at the Ministry of Civil Affairs, argues that farmers have more interests that conflict with the state—and with each other. They are land-owners. They are more heavily taxed than city-dwellers. They resent those taxes when the money is badly spent or disappears into the pockets of local officials. In other words, says Mr Wang, "democracy is about interests, discussing concrete things like salaries, taxes, building roads, resolving conflicts. It's not about shouting slogans like 'Overthrow the government! Down with [the former prime minister] Li Peng!'" Farmers may understand this better than city folk, but that is changing as the state-controlled economy is dismantled. "Look at all the problems in Beijing," says Mr Wang, waving a hand to the window, "pollution, traffic chaos, construction. Democracy is about the recontrol of government. When city people say that if peasants can organise elections, we should too, I say: 'no problem.'" Wider democracy, in short, has already become the open agenda of some in government.

This suggests that a new compact between government and people may start to be redrawn sooner than many think. Indeed, in the debate over when and on what terms China should join the WTO, the western world should perhaps not exaggerate its ability to shape the course of China's political development, either for good or ill. Yet nor should it underestimate the dangers if China cannot change, or cannot change peacefully. China cannot get very far towards political reform without confronting new demands to revise the verdict on Tiananmen. But that the Communist Party will be loth to do. And it's recourse in such trying times—a prickly chauvinism—would surely be felt beyond China's borders.

The Chinese Government Crushes Student
Demonstrations in Tiananmen Square:
June 4, 1989

The Scene in Tiananmen Square on June 4, 1989

by Louise Doder

The following article by Louise Doder, a writer for *Maclean's* magazine, was published just days after the crackdown on student demonstrations in Tiananmen Square on June 4, 1989. Like many initial accounts of the event, Doder's story describes soldiers firing into the crowds in the square and killing many student demonstrators. Subsequent accounts contradict this version of events and indicate that the majority of the victims were nonstudent protesters who were killed as troops passed through Beijing suburbs on their way to the square.

In the middle of one night last week, a group of students transported three huge pieces of plaster and wood—loaded on bicycles—into Beijing's Tiananmen Square. Forming a cordon against the secret police who tried to intervene, the rebellious students painstakingly put the sections together and erected an instant icon: a home-made, 35-foot-high replica of the Statue of Liberty. The students christened it the "Goddess of Democracy." But early on Sunday, what had been largely a peaceful mass occupation for four weeks changed dramatically when thousands of armed troops marched on the square, crushing the rebellion in a deadly showdown with the defiant demonstrators, and left a bloodbath in their wake. Said a crying worker, huddled in the square: "I have just had my last cigarette. We are going to die."

The troops forced their way into Tiananmen behind armored personnel carriers and tanks. They first fired off tracer bullets and tear gas, while loudspeaker messages warned the tens of thousands of students to leave. Then, they opened fire directly on the crowds and charged them with bayonets, killing—according to initial reports—hundreds of demonstrators, leaving hundreds of others wounded and causing mass panic. Some students responded by hurling ignited bottles of gasoline at the troops. Meanwhile, ambulances, their sirens wailing, carried most of the injured to nearby hospitals. Bicycles, pedicabs and city buses were also pressed into service to move the dead and wounded.

"Bandits, Bandits!"

In the early stages of the showdown, the students had remained orderly and they swiftly threw up barricades, which the armored vehicles systematically smashed. They even managed to surround and burn two of the vehicles. But when the soldiers began firing randomly from all sides and from the roof of the Great Hall of the People on the western side of the square, fear and confusion spread. The huge crowds desperately sought safety in the side streets leading from Tiananmen, shouting "Bandits, bandits!" Even there, the troops continued to fire on them, as screams of terror filled the area. One man, who had been wounded and treated in a casualty ward—where he said the floor was inches deep in blood—added, "They were simply raking the crowd with bullets."

The massive military intervention clearly surprised the students and their supporters and suggested a long period of future instability. In the early stages of the intervention, the students showed remarkable courage in the face of the armed troops, and the army's ability to exert control without the use of extreme force seemed to be virtually nonexistent. When they first tried to invade the square on Saturday morning, the students scored a dramatic victory by forming a human barricade and turning the soldiers back with chants of "Are you human?" and "Do you have a conscience?"

But when the army started to return the next time, about 12

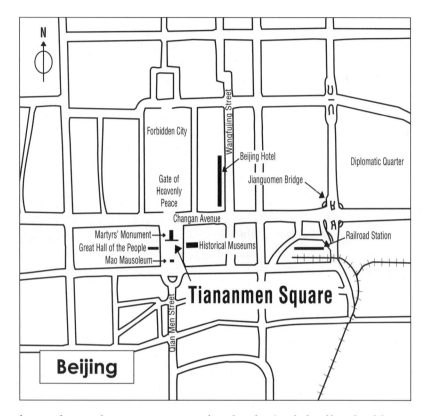

hours later, there was no turning back. And the line had been clearly drawn between the students and their supporters demonstrating for more democracy, and the forces of the conservative government of Premier Li Peng and the senior leader Deng Xiaoping. Said one woman protester, who claimed to be married to a soldier in the square: "The People's Army has become a fascist army, pointing guns at their own people." Added a hysterical man in Beijing's Shuili Hospital: "We can never forgive the Communist party for this."

The students' protest began with prodemocracy demonstrations following the death on April 15 of former Communist party chairman Hu Yaobang, whom they regarded as a reformer. It gained momentum in May when Soviet leader Mikhail Gorbachev arrived in Beijing—the first such visit in 30 years—and the students hailed him as a political revolutionary. On May 13, just two days before Gorbachev's visit, 1,000 students—the number later grew to 3,000—began a hunger strike on the square. By May 17, a million people had packed Tiananmen and the demonstrations spread throughout the country. But by the middle of last week, following the declaration of martial law on May 20, the number of students in the square had dropped to 2,000 tired and hungry protesters. Then the demonstrators hauled in the "Goddess of Democracy," and, later, the troops invaded.

World Reaction

The terror in Tiananmen created sharp reactions in world capitals. President George Bush [Senior] said, "I deeply deplore the decision to use force against peaceful demonstrators and the consequent loss of life." In Ottawa, External Affairs Minister Joe Clark called on the Chinese government to "cease its military action and to return to peaceful methods to resolve the current crisis." He added, "We greatly regret that, following a period of evident restraint, the Chinese authorities initiated the use of force."

The army's stunning and ultimately successful intervention was unexpected partly because earlier in the week there had been continuing signs of the government's reluctance to follow through on its earlier declaration of martial law and other stringent measures. The foreign media had widely ignored a government imposition of nearly a total news blackout. Authorities arrested and then released three union leaders after 2,000 people protested their detention. And when the government sponsored rallies against the uprising—at which marchers were reportedly paid to chant "Smash the traitorous bandits into little pieces"—the participants were decidedly unenthusiastic. But on Sunday morning in Tiananmen Square, it was the demonstrators and their statue that had been crushed. The government was very definitely in control—and a massacre was the result.

The Destruction of the Berlin Wall Signals the Start of Eastern European Revolution

by John Rossant

In 1989 the world was still divided into the spheres of influence that had been drawn up by the victors of World War II. On one side, the United States and its Western European allies held to the notions of free-market economies and democratic political systems. On the other side, the Soviet Union and its Eastern European satellites still extolled the virtues of communism. The Berlin Wall stood as a powerful symbolic dividing line as well as a very real physical barrier between these two worlds, and, although the Warsaw Pact nations suffered from chronic shortages of goods and stagnant economies, few informed observers believed that political affairs would change much in the foreseeable future. In June 1989, however, voters in Poland put an end to more than forty years of Communist rule.

When it became apparent that Soviet leader Mikhail Gorbachev would not order Russian tanks to crush Poland's break with communism (the Soviet Union had crushed similar demonstrations of political free will in Hungary and Czechoslovakia in the past) other

John Rossant, "Europe Ten Years Later," *Business Week*, November 8, 1999, p. 56. Copyright © 1999 by McGraw-Hill, Inc. Reproduced by permission.

Eastern bloc nations began to agitate for freedom. When the wave of reform reached East Germany, crowds in East Berlin gathered at the most recognizable symbol of Communist repression, the Berlin Wall, to demand their freedom and to implore their leaders to open the gates to democratic West Germany. On November 9, 1989, East German officials could no longer deny the crowds gathering at the Berlin Wall; at 10:30 P.M. they opened the gates. Jubilant easterners spilled into the streets of West Berlin, joyously celebrating with their countrymen. When the wall fell, the dam was breached. One by one, like a line of dominoes, Eastern bloc nations shook off their Communist regimes. By 1990 the Berlin Wall was nothing more than a reminder of a bygone era, Germany was reunited, and communism in Europe was dead. By the summer of 1991 the wave of reform had swept all the way to Moscow itself, where a failed coup hastened the death of the Communist Party and the death of the Soviet Union itself.

In the following essay written in 1999, ten years after the fall of the Berlin Wall, journalist John Rossant asserts that the event not only announced the death of communism in Europe, but it also heralded the death of old Europe and signaled a new beginning for the West. Where state bureaucrats once ruled, businessmen, artists, and entrepreneurs have taken charge. Where dedication to Communist containment once dominated, commitment to economic prosperity now rules. Though certain tensions and instabilities have arisen from the change, Rossant contends that the Westernization of Europe's politics and economy has had enormous benefits. Eastern Europe has provided a massive labor pool and lucrative new markets for many companies, and European business now has endless opportunities to grow.

In addition to fostering economic prosperity, Rossant contends that the collapse of the Berlin Wall hastened the unification of Europe. In the absence of the Cold War's threats of Communist takeovers, many Western European governments were able to shore up their budgets, tackle corruption, and better prepare for economic unification (the euro debuted in 1999). As exciting as these changes have been, Rossant contends that it is only the beginning. The absence of the Communist specter is providing a fertile ground in which European prosperity can continue to grow.

Already it seems like another era, another epoch. And it was. Take Checkpoint Charlie on Friedrichstrasse in the center of Berlin, in the heart of a once-divided Europe. Until Nov. 9, 1989, it demarcated a world that now seems far away: the East German klieg lights, the fearsome Todesstreifen, or "death-strip" of no-man's-land, and most of all, that relentless stretch of 13-foot-high reinforced concrete—the Berlin Wall. The Wall was a stark symbol of the 20th century, of the horrors of its world wars and the clash of its ideologies.

Look at this intersection of Friedrichstrasse today. A resplendent Berlin is once again the capital of a united Germany. The Wall has been swept away, as have the barbed wire and the guard towers. Long forgotten are the trigger-happy East German border guards and the growls of their police dogs.

And exactly where the grim checkpoint once stood, a new building is about to rise: Berlin Checkpoint Charlie Plaza, an ultra-modern eight-story office tower that promises future tenants the latest in high-speed data connections. "For information," a big sign says in English, "see our Web site: www.Checkpoint-Charlie.com." If ever a metaphor were needed for the world's technological and political transformation in the past decade, it might be that very sign.

The fall of the Berlin Wall not only heralded the extraordinary collapse of the Communist order from the Elbe to the Urals, a system that once seemed both monolithic and eternal. It also symbolized an epochal turning point for the West—and Western Europe in particular.

Mental Blocks

It was nothing less than the end of the old Europe. Also collapsing with those 66 miles of concrete were the many mental and political barriers built up over the Cold War. "The fall of the Wall set off forces in Europe which were unprecedented in history," says Raymond Seitz, Assistant Secretary of State for Europe in 1989 and now vice-chairman of Lehman Brothers Inc.

Make no mistake: The 21st century may formally begin on Jan. 1, 2000, but in terms of a fresh way of looking at things, the new century kicked off on Nov. 9, 1989, when thousands of jubilant East Berliners breached the Wall that had long divided their city.

Now, [in 1999], a new economic and political architecture is emerging from the rubble. The result is a much more vibrant and pluralistic Continent—one in which the state is no longer the final arbiter of society. The driving forces are technology and business, rather than ideology and geopolitics. Businesspeople, artists, local officials, and not the least, entrepreneurs, have overtaken national politicians as the Continent's key decision makers.

It is they who will have to confront the next decade's greatest challenge: truly integrating the former East Bloc countries into the European fold. The political pressure is now clearly on to bring in countries such as Poland, Hungary, and the Czech Republic within the next five years or so. But enlargement could not only create economic tensions as poorer, less efficient economies join the European Union (EU); it also stands to change the very nature of Europe by moving the center of gravity further east.

Some see a silver lining, pointing to the spectacular economic success enjoyed in the EU by such former economic basket cases as Ireland and Portugal. Central Europe has sophisticated and

A graffiti-covered section of the Berlin Wall. The wall was brought down in November 1989, reuniting East and West Germany.

well-educated populations and pent-up consumer demand. "In many ways," says Dirk Hurdig, secretary general of UNICE, the European employers' federation, "Central European countries are better positioned than Asian tigers."

The Battle in the West

Back in the wealthier West, the battle for a new Europe is not over. Labor markets are still rigid, so workers tend not to go where the jobs are. The welfare state remains fiercely protected by politicians, trade unions, millions of voters, and vulnerable businesses that fear a completely free market. Germany itself is now a key battleground. Europe's largest economy, which has spent $560 billion on reunification, is now struggling with the need to cut back social spending to make its economy more competitive. In the East, meanwhile, even the strongest economies have yet to build the legal framework needed to protect investors and workers from the worst excesses of unbridled capitalism.

For millions in Europe, it's an understandably frightening new world where jobs can be easily lost and the old certainties have vanished.

But the momentum of events unleashed in 1989 keeps dictating change, while new communications technology has been accelerating the pace. Central Europe's opening made millions of skilled, low-cost workers available to Western companies seeking new bases of operation and new markets. With the forces of globalization at Western Europe's doorstep, workers in France and Germany could no longer rely on protection from cheap Asian imports, especially with Czechs and Poles hungry for work just a few hundred miles away.

The fall of the Wall also hastened the unification of Western Europe. Of course, Europe's political leaders had already been groping their way toward greater unity before 1989. By the mid-1980s, much of Western Europe had already embarked on pushing through a single market. And Spain and Portugal finally joined the European Community in 1986.

But the Wall's collapse galvanized the entire Continent, accelerating a united Europe as nothing had before. With the sudden crumbling of the Cold War's iron certainties, Europe needed new reasons to hang together. And with Germany reunified, other Europeans had to be quickly reassured of "a European Germany rather than a German Europe," as then-Chancellor Helmut Kohl put it. Despite German voters' deep skepticism of a plan to do away with their stable Deutschemark, Kohl threw his prestige behind European Monetary Union. He and other Western European leaders had already been negotiating an agreement that would lay out the framework for economic union. In short order, they inked the historic Maastricht Treaty of 1992. By January, 1999, the euro, Europe's common currency, was born.

The End of Politics-as-Usual

In a few short years, the factors dominating European political and economic life had completely changed. The need to prepare for monetary union forced governments to tackle their budget deficits. And as the threat of Soviet-led communism disappeared, the politics-as-usual of the old Europe went through a profound transformation.

In Italy, where the West's largest communist party had been shut out of power for four decades, successive Christian Democrat and Socialist governments had created institutionalized corruption. Now, crusading anti-corruption judges like Antonio Di Pietro could go on the offensive without exposing the country to a communist takeover. Di Pietro was soon snaring powerful politicians like ex-Prime Minister Bettino Craxi. By 1994, an entire generation of Italian politicians was forcibly retired. Likewise in France the anti-corruption drive started to expose the shady dealings of the government and business elite.

As the old politicians have faded from the scenes—and with them, Europe's clubby, old-boy capitalism—younger ones have emerged willing to give market forces freer play. That has set the stage for unprecedented market deregulation and privatization. Even if the many center-left leaders disguise this . . . by calling it "flexibility" and "freeing up resources," there is no mistaking the effects. France, which nationalized the commercial banking system in 1982, had made a 180-degree turn by 1991. Banks, manufacturers, and insurers have all gone on the block.

Italy has witnessed perhaps the most dramatic shift. It started the 1990s with 90% of its banking system and 60% of its economy in state hands. Now, as the decade draws to a close, most banking is in private hands and almost all state industry has been sold off. In economic terms at least, says Carlo De Benedetti, the former chairman of Olivetti, "Italy was probably the biggest beneficiary of the fall of the Wall."

With the adoption of the euro [in January 1999], the full impact of 1989 is in some ways only now being felt. "After the Wall," says Marco Tronchetti Provera, chief executive of tiremaker Pirelli, "the single European market became a possible reality. And in the last 24 months, it has become reality."

Deals, Deals

Thus companies are swiftly knitting together a real Continental economy. Mergers and acquisitions are remaking the corporate landscape. The value of deals is approaching $1.3 trillion [in 1999], up fourfold from [1994], according to J.P. Morgan & Co.

Once politically sacrosanct sectors are fast opening up. Since deregulation two years ago, the telecoms industry has become a no-holds-barred battleground. In October alone, Germany's Mannesmann launched a $32 billion buyout of Britain's Orange PLC, while France Telecom ponied up $9 billion for a chunk of Germany's E-Plus Mobilfunk.

The ferment in business has produced a new icon in Europe: the CEO. From DaimlerChrysler's Jurgen Schrempp to French media mogul Jean-Marie Messier, corporate chieftains swagger like rock stars in today's Europe. Old-guard politicians like France's late President Francois Mitterrand were once masters at courting such attention. Today, "the heroes are entrepreneurs going to Silicon Valley and making it big," says French political scientist Dominique Moisi.

Another upstart on the scene: the shareholder. Now that many European equities are traded in euros—not local currencies—it's much easier for institutional investors to compare stocks and figure out which managers are lagging behind their peers. From the CalPERS pension fund [in California] to unit trusts based in Edinburgh, fund managers are pressing for the returns—and the kind of corporate governance—that once could only be gotten on Wall Street. "My capital is now diversified, and I've got institutional shareholders in places like the U.S. and Britain as well as France," says Thierry Desmarest, CEO of French oil giant TotalFina. It was those shareholders—and not the French government—who threw their firepower behind Desmarest's successful $44 billion bid last July to take over rival French group Elf Aquitaine. Desmarest, who also engineered the first big cross-border takeover in Europe's energy industry, is quick to acknowledge that in Western Europe today, borders simply matter less. Of course, multinationals such as Unilever, Citibank, and Royal Dutch/Shell Group had long pursued global strategies. But after the Wall came down, "the leading 40,000 corporations made the significant discovery that the world was now their oyster. Political inhibitions simply didn't exist anymore," says Jonathan Story, professor at Fontainebleau-based INSEAD. The result of that sea change has been an explosion in cross-border investment. According to the U.N.'s World Investment Report issued [in] August [1999], total foreign direct investment flows rose from $90 billion in 1992 to more than $400 billion [in 1999].

Big companies in Europe are not the only ones enjoying new-found freedom. Smaller outfits, especially in high tech, are starting to multiply. With the rising popularity of the Neuer Markt, Internet stock offerings are multiplying—and changing the mind-set of a new generation. Engineering grads, turning away from safe bets such as Ericsson and Siemens, are launching their own outfits. "Most of my classmates are looking for investors," says 25-year-old Jacob Hamacher, CEO of Ehand, a Stockholm mobile telephony startup.

"It Is a New World"

People like Hamacher show that there's also a generational effect at play. With the end of the Cold War and its nuclear dooms-day scenarios, young people no longer dwell on the limitations of history. The Wall "influenced my entire existence," says 52-year-old German economist Hans-Werner Sinn, a top authority on events leading to its collapse. Today, his students at the University of Munich are indifferent to the events of 1989. "They are the Internet generation, the generation that is traveling every-where," says Sinn. "It is a new world."

Red Flags

Well, not entirely. The forces of pre-1989 are still playing a role. The hard-left French Communist Party can still bring out 50,000 protesters in central Paris, as it did in a mid-October [1999] demonstration to push the government to create jobs. More hammer and sickles and red flags floated down Boulevard Hauss-mann than are ever seen nowadays in Moscow.

Germany shows the ambivalence many Europeans feel about the world they have created since 1989. The country courageously embraced the challenge of reunification. But no one in the political class dared to push for an economic revolution to accompany the political one. Instead, Germany has largely preserved its old economic model at a time of global change. "We spent billions trying to build an old-style industrial economy in East Germany," says Hasso Plattner, chief of German software giant SAP. "Meanwhile, America was building a whole new economy in California." This represents a huge opportunity lost.

Yet the impact of the Wall's collapse on European attitudes has been so tremendous that, for the first time, there is hope for even more radical change. The consequences of 1989 are still being felt, and in some respects, Europe cannot afford to stay put. Its governments are slowly running out of money to support the old welfare state, and taxes cannot get any higher. Perhaps the only alternative is to widen the economic and political freedoms still gaining strength. More cross-border mergers, more market-opening moves by governments, more opportunities for restless entrepreneurs and politicians who want to break with the past: These are all part of Europe today. The first decade was just a start.

The Scene at the Berlin Wall in November 1989

by Elizabeth Pond

In the following essay Elizabeth Pond, a journalist who was in Berlin when the wall fell, describes the jubilant atmosphere as tentative East German guards finally opened the gates to West Germany. Pond points out that the opening of the Berlin Wall inspired East Germans to demand more freedoms of their government. Though the freedoms were eventually granted, Pond asserts that they were not enough to prevent the collapse of communism in Germany. Within a year Germany would be reunited and communism in Eastern Europe would be dead. Elizabeth Pond is author of *Beyond the Wall: Germany's Road to Unification*, from which this essay is excerpted.

W hen the Berlin Wall fell, the crash obliterated a country, an empire, and an era. The fall redeemed the failed revolution of 1848, Europe's cavalier slide into war in 1914, and [Nazi leader Adolf] Hitler's rise to power in 1933. It lifted the specter of nuclear holocaust, yet expanded the paradoxical long peace the balance of terror had bestowed on a quarrelsome Europe. For the first time since romantic demons were loosed among the Germans, it sealed their Western identity and began to heal their right-left schism. It united them once more, this time benignly, and demystified their existential questions

Elizabeth Pond, *Beyond the Wall: Germany's Road to Unification*. Washington, DC: The Brookings Institution, 1993. Copyright © 1993 by The Twentieth Century Fund, Inc. Reproduced by permission of the publisher.

into the more tolerable politics of everyday bickering. Mischievously, it let the United States drop its fixation on its superpower twin, hold up a mirror to its domestic self, and recoil. More malignly, the wall's disappearance dissolved the old pax sovietica into ancient blood feuds.

The Wall Comes Down

The upheaval began with an announcement that East German Politburo member Günter Schabowski made one Thursday, just in time for the evening television news. Henceforth, he let drop at the end of an hour's rambling press conference, East Germans could cross the border into West Germany.

There was utter confusion as to what he actually meant. Many East Germans thought that the thousands of emigrants who were deserting the German Democratic Republic (GDR) via the hole that had recently opened in Czechoslovakia could now go directly to the Federal Republic of Germany. Others surmised that the East-West German border proper—excluding the infamous wall sealing the enclave of West Berlin off from surrounding East Germany—was now open. Still others tentatively took his words to mean that at last East Germans, who had been cooped up in the bleak Soviet bloc for four decades, could all travel freely.

The Politburo itself—or, more precisely, Schabowski and fledgling party General Secretary Egon Krenz, the Politburo's only two functioning members after the GDR's paralyzed old guard had been dumped the day before—apparently did intend to open all border crossings, but only in coming days and only in a bureaucratic fashion, with stamped visas for most, but continued rejection for some.

Within minutes of the proclamation, however, intent was irrelevant. A popular "explosion," as one East German official described it, occurred. East Berliners rushed to the exits to West Berlin that had been barred to them for twenty-eight years—and found them still barred. This time, though, they did not just abandon the attempt and docilely go home. Instead, they planted themselves in place. They were used to standing in line, and they were patient, but they insisted with growing vehemence—and with swelling reinforcements and ever more Western television crews recording each gesture—that the armed, but vastly outnumbered, border guards let them pass. "Open the gate! Open the gate!" chanted the throng at Bornholmer Strasse, then added, as a good-humored promise, that if they were allowed this taste of the West they would still return to the GDR: "We'll come back! We'll come back!"

The date was November 9, 1989, the fifty-first anniversary of Hitler's Kristallnacht rampage against the synagogues, and the seventy-first anniversary of imperial Germany's collapse in World War I.

The rollercoaster of emotions that night went from a collective leap of joy, to deep-seated dread, to stubborn determination, then back to ecstasy. Even as the East Berliners began their vigil, the West German Bundestag heard the news and spontaneously broke into singing the national anthem. For whatever reason— awe, premonition, or perhaps a yearning for a new life for their Eastern brothers and sisters—this time the Green members of parliament did not walk out at such a display of national sentiment. The moment of truth had come, when the Westerners could only wait and watch and sing.

For more than three hours the crowds and the tension mounted as the standoff dragged on at the checkpoints between East and West Berlin. Then some taunts rang out, and some pushing and shoving erupted between East Berliners at the front of the pack and the border guards they confronted nose to nose.

The city's Soviet and Western military commanders—the four victorious powers of World War II were still legally responsible for the security of Berlin and of "Germany as a whole"—worried about the volatile situation. They contacted one another and stayed in constant touch throughout that night and the next few days to avoid dangerous misunderstandings. At any moment, they feared, tempers might flare or someone might panic as the irresistible force met the immovable object. No one was sure how the GDR border troops, the National People's Army (NVA), the *Stasi* (East Germany's secret police), or even the Soviet KGB might react. Ultimately, "the choice was either to let them through or shoot," explained a senior allied officer in West Berlin.

The Gates Are Opened

By 10:30 P.M., the ranking East German border guards at Bornholmer Strasse and three other crossing points in the center of the city—still facing the crowds and still lacking instructions— made their unthinkable choice. These servants of the most rigidly Prussian code of obedience and hierarchy in the entire Soviet bloc took authority into their own hands and opened the gates.

The dike was breached. The flood could no longer be held back. By 11 P.M. East German Interior Minister Friedrich Dickel acknowledged the fait accompli and confirmed the local commanders' desperate decision with an official order.

The multitude spilled through the openings. Suspense exploded into revelry. Western hosts, joining the fairy tale come true, dashed to the spots where East Berliners were pouring in, showered chocolate and carnations and gummibears on their guests, thumped their two-stroke Trabant cars in welcome, and even called the Trabis' nitrous plumes the perfume of freedom. Eyes shone. Tears flowed unashamedly. Total strangers embraced. New friends deluged each other with champagne. They shouted, sang, danced, ran, skipped, played, effervesced. Then, as one, they exorcised the wall forever by transforming it from a prison to a stage. In front of the Brandenburg Gate they clambered on top of it, and kept finding room to haul up yet another person, as in some gigantic circus trick. "The wall must fall," they chanted. "We shall overcome," they sang.

Even the GDR border guards and NVA troops were swept up in the jubilation, metamorphosing instantly from jailers to fellow celebrants. Here one officer accepted flowers tucked into his rifle. There another sheepishly gave away his hat to a girl who asked for it and won a kiss in return. At the Brandenburg Gate a third initially held fast to the cordon blocking public access, then succumbed to the anguish and tears of a grandmother who wanted just once in her life to walk to this symbol of Berlin, and escorted her there himself. Transfixed, the entire world watched the drama.

Early on, a few people standing on the "antifascist defense wall" started hammering at it as if they really meant to demolish it. At that point the East German police finally intervened with water cannon. Yet even this display of force was half-hearted: the law enforcers elevated the trajectory so that the jet would not blast all the roustabouts off the wall with full impact and possible injury, and left one grinning Berliner perched on the crest with his umbrella raised as a shield against the torrent.

The British, who administered the sector in the heart of the city, took no chances. They dispatched a military band to play at the wall, not only to help ease the atmosphere, but also to keep an inconspicuous eye on things. To avert any risky buildup of idle crowds in the formerly deserted Reichstag grounds that were now the focus of the events, they provided unmarked buses to shuttle passengers to and fro. To avoid the need for British riot control operations that might set off an international incident, they authorized the West Berlin police to enter the no-man's strip of East German territory west of the wall for the first time in twenty-eight years. Thus it was German police who prevented West Berliners fired by a generation's cumulative rage—or perhaps only the adrenaline of the moment—from tearing down their own segment of wall and bursting through to challenge the police on the other side.

The improvisation worked. In the end, the British band did not have to drop its trombones to contain violence, there were no *Stasi* provocations, and Berliners' suppressed wrath was engulfed by the new exuberance. In the next few days the wall avengers mellowed into wall woodpeckers, chiseling souvenirs out of the ugliest and now most superfluous piece of architecture in Berlin. One cyclist even rode atop the wall. His feat lay less in keeping his balance on the straight and narrow than in finding that rare moment when his way was not totally blocked by bodies.

As the novel relaxation spread throughout the GDR, one eleven-year-old in Karl Marx Stadt rushed home from school to tell his parents the fantastic news that his teacher had said "good morning" when she entered the classroom, and the class too had responded with "good morning" (instead of the rote exchange of "be prepared," "always prepared"). A nine-year-old Leipziger, asked to write about the most exciting experience in his life, described the adventure as his family drove into West Germany and the border guard actually smiled at them. And in fulfillment of every child's dream, the government canceled Saturday classes for the rest of the year, as so many pupils and teachers would otherwise be playing hooky in the Federal Republic.

The Happiest People on Earth

On November 10, in front of his city hall, West Berlin Mayor Walter Momper told the first joint gathering of East and West Berliners in decades that Germans were now the happiest people on earth. Willy Brandt, the city's mayor when the wall sprang up in 1961, the West German chancellor who began *Ostpolitik* (Eastern policy) détente in 1969, and now, after a lifetime of partisan battles, the avuncular elder statesman, seconded the view of his fellow Social Democrat. "What belongs together is now growing together," he proclaimed. Only conservative foes were churlish enough to remind him that shortly before the eruption in the GDR, Brandt himself had dismissed the Christian Democrats' striving for one Germany as a "life-long delusion."

Chancellor Helmut Kohl, who over the years had promoted that life-long delusion more doggedly than any other politician, was also on the podium, having interrupted a visit to Poland to be present at the making of history. He expected no immediate reward from his lightning trip. On the contrary, he anticipated the heckling he had to suffer from a group of West Berlin leftists. With an eye on the general election a year away, however, he was determined to avoid Konrad Adenauer's mistake of 1961. Then the first West German chancellor, deferring to the Western allies' request for restraint, had decided not to visit the beleaguered city after the Berlin Wall went up overnight. In consequence, he had taken a drubbing in the next election.

In the course of the rally, Kohl at least had the mixed satisfaction of receiving an urgent message from Soviet President Mikhail Gorbachev asking the chancellor to try to calm down public passions in East as well as in West Berlin. Kohl welcomed Gorbachev's acknowledgment of a certain West German authority in East Berlin and implicit recognition that unification would be the central issue. He worried, however, that the KGB or *Stasi* might be inciting Gorbachev to let the tanks roll by feeding him disinformation portraying the peaceful crowds as unruly. Kohl therefore stressed to Gorbachev that everything was under control and that a happy festival spirit prevailed. The West Germans' concern that Gorbachev's message held a veiled warning was allayed only by the friendly phone conversation between Gorbachev and Kohl on November 11.

Oblivious to this or any other threat for the first time in half a century, ordinary Germans continued their festival over the weekend. Easterners ate free pea soup; drank free beer; attended West German soccer games, rock concerts, and the Berlin Philharmonic for free; picked up their DM 100 "welcome gifts" from West German banks that had stayed open on Saturday and Sunday; and then bought Walkmans and jeans jackets at shops that had also been excused from adhering to the strict legal closing hours. They rode without tickets on West Berlin subways in densities approaching Tokyo levels. They collected free city maps and coffee, and that ultimate symbol of unattainability, bananas.

A few had the good fortune to hear Mstislav Rostropovich, who sped to Checkpoint Charlie to play his beloved Bach cello suites there alfresco. Many more would later hear Leonard Bernstein conduct Beethoven's Ninth Symphony, and in artistic license that no German would dare take, change *Freude* (joy) to *Freiheit* (freedom) in the sacred Schiller text.

"We found we weren't so different after all," mused one East Berlin communist who lived two minutes away from the wall, but had never before set foot in West Berlin.

Soon he would change his mind, and so would disgruntled Western taxpayers. Yet he uttered a truth for those few extraordinary days of personal unification. In those magical hours Germans discovered not only that they could be as spontaneous as Latins, but also that they really were one people. West Germans, who had tended to support reunification in the abstract while finding their poor relations something of a burden in the flesh, realized that they really did care a great deal about their brothers and sisters. East Germans, who had half feared the West's chaos and violence, were dazzled instead by the casual opulence and generosity they encountered.

Three Weeks That Shook Off the Party

Afterward, the East German communists tried to patch Humpty Dumpty together again. Many different metaphors occurred to the various embarrassed observers of the disintegration, who for years had agreed that the GDR regime was entrenched and formidable. Some now called it a house of cards; others said it had been a grand building with an imposing facade that was suddenly found to be rotten at the core. "We created ruins without weapons," any number of East Germans began saying, not only a sardonic reference to the collapse of institutions and the physical decay of buildings unrepaired for half a century, but also a pun on the peace movement's slogan: "Create peace without weapons."

Civil society now reasserted itself against politics, then came to determine politics. Inside and outside the ruling party, pluralism burgeoned and political actors proliferated. To begin with, cracks appeared between rivals—in this case, Krenz and Schabowski—as is typical of an unstable succession period in a one-party system. Then institutionally, responsibility devolved from the incapacitated party to the government under reforming Prime Minister Hans Modrow. The somnolent parliament and nominally noncommunist "bloc parties" were revitalized. And in a conflict of generations, younger communists revolted and took to the new political fashion in their own mass demonstrations for the acceleration of Socialist Unity (Communist) party reforms.

On Friday, the day after the wall opened, Krenz continued his earlier strategy of limited reforms from above just as if his whole world had not fractured. From the Central Committee he got formal approval for his action program proposing economic liberalization, freedom of assembly and association, and free, secret elections with multiple candidates. Under the program, discussion within the Socialist Unity party (SED) was to be broadened, but once decisions had been made, the discipline of democratic centralism from above would still prevail.

As so often since Krenz had been propelled into office three weeks before, it was too little too late. Four full or candidate members of his new Politburo had to give up their posts immediately because they were voted down in an unprecedented revolt by their local party organizations. Some 150,000 Communist party members again gathered outside the Central Committee building to protest the SED's slow evolution and to demand a full party congress in December with powers to dismiss the old Central Committee. Krenz's royal gesture in coming out to talk to them and assure them that the leadership understood the problems, instead of mollifying them, only infuriated them.

By Sunday the reshuffled Politburo gave in and approved a party congress. The West and East Berlin mayors shook hands at the new crossing point hacked out at Potsdamer Platz, the most egregious example of the wall's ruthless slicing through the heart of a neighborhood, separating two generations of children from their local park. The Interior Ministry announced that in the past three days it had already issued 4.3 million passports for travel to the West.

"The Wall in Our Heads"

On Monday campaigns for the first ever open elections of delegates began in local party units. In Leipzig 200,000 people, unpacified and undiverted by the new lure of the golden West, turned up at the regular Monday prayers and demonstration. Docent Christoph Kähler, preaching in the Nikolai Church, could not resist the clear parallel of Biblical Jericho: "When the trumpets sounded on the seventh day, the walls fell, of their own accord. A miracle!" he exclaimed. "On seven Mondays the Leipzigers encircled the city and called, '*Wir sind das Volk*' [We are the people]. Then the wall fell, of its own accord, but, thank God, without violence. That is our peaceful revolution, a miracle. . . .

"But still [another wall] has fallen, the wall in our heads. That is the division between our own real opinion and what we dared say. That is the caution that we learned as children, then transmitted further to our children, in order to protect them. That is the game of hiding our thoughts, a game that relegated our most important political thinking to the arts and the church rather than the marketplace or city hall, where it actually belonged."

Some activists had worried that the heady bread and circuses of bananas and free travel would sap political discontent and allow the old regime to reconsolidate. Instead, the maxim that the worst time for tyrants is when they improve things held true. Far from satisfying people who had felt victimized by the regime, reforms only raised their expectations and inspired the beneficiaries to ask for more. On November 13, just as on November 6, the Leipzig crowds poured out of the Nikolai Church to make the next set of radicalized demands that Krenz would never catch up with.

Parliament Rejuvenated

Yet as the East Germans now turned from the elemental yearning for travel, free elections, and throwing the bums out and progressed to more complex choices about how to structure their new polity, the Leipzig Mondays in the Nikolai Church could no longer function adequately as the national town meeting. The first substitute consisted of the legislature and bloc parties that for forty years had been the SED's puppets. Gingerly at first, and then in a rush, these began shedding their obeisance to the SED's leading role, as enshrined in article 1 of the constitution.

The Liberals and the Democratic Farmers party sounded out the dissidents' New Forum and other fledgling political clubs with proposals of cooperation, and were scorned. The Christian Democrats ejected Gerald Götting, the communist clone who had run the party for decades, and selected as its less malleable new chairman Lothar de Maizìre, an erstwhile professional violist, a lawyer who had defended dissenters, a vice president of the Protestant Synod, and the GDR's unlikely future prime minister. He wrestled with his decision all night before accepting, he said, but in the end agreed to do his part to ensure that the next generation of children would no longer have to lie, to be "Janus-headed and double-toungued."

As the bloc parties quickened in mid-November, the SED decayed. Many local communist officials resigned, were kicked out, or, in at least three cases, committed suicide. The old communist leaders of the Free German Trade Union, the Free German Youth, and all the other mass organizations were deposed, along with the old editors of the party newspapers. Hundreds of thousands of members quit the party; within months the rolls would shrink from 2.3 million to some 700,000. The rolls of the Free German Youth also dropped, from close to 2 million to some 1 million. Not even the abruptly begun party expulsions and prosecution of old Politburo members, nor the equally abrupt rehabilitation of victims of Stalinism, could restore the party's reputation.

Parliament, which had met for only a few days every year, and until November had unanimously passed every resolution but one presented to it by the SED, now began to flex some muscle. After four weeks of ignored demands for its convening from individual Volkskammer delegates and the new grass-roots organizations, parliament finally met on Monday, November 13, and staged one unprecedented scene after another. Horst Sindermann, speaker for thirteen years, resigned. The Volkskammer promptly elected a new presidium, voting for the first time with secret ballots, and held the first real debate in its history. The just-deposed strongman of eighteen years, Erich Honecker, his wife Margot, and twenty-five other SED deputies gave up their seats. The remaining deputies suddenly began grilling various officials, including Sindermann and the outgoing prime minister of twenty-two years, Willi Stoph. They extracted from Finance Minister Ernst Höfner the previously classified information that firms in the GDR had 130 billion ost marks of internal debts (though at this point they could not yet extract the crucial figure of external debt, later revealed as $20.6 billion, double previous official figures).

The Volkskammer even insisted on questioning the dreaded Erich Mielke, minister for state security for the past thirty-two years. Never before had the eighty-two-year-old felt obliged to report to parliament. Now the man who had administered the whole poisonous system of internal spying automatically addressed his listeners as comrades, and could not grasp why the noncommunist delegates bridled at this appellation. Grotesquely he justified himself with the explanation, "But I love you all!"

Derisive laughter filled the chamber and the living rooms of those watching on television.

Many Germans watching Mielke's stumbling performance even concluded that he was senile. West German intelligence officers who interviewed him a year later did not share this view, and saw in his Volkskammer presentation a deliberate, spirited defense of the *Stasi*. In his parliamentary remarks, Mielke complained bitterly that party and government leaders had ignored all the excellent information his ministry had given them about unrest in the country in 1989. "We presented it. Believe me! Believe me! We did present it to them," he protested. "The only problem is that much of what we reported was not taken into consideration, was not appreciated."

On Tuesday, November 14, censorship was lifted in the GDR. . . .

On Friday, November 17, in his maiden speech, Prime Minister Modrow promised that his government would institute even more far-reaching political, legal, economic, environmental, educational, and administrative reforms than Krenz had already done, with greater transparency and accountability. He wanted to do everything possible, Modrow said, "so that the democratic renewal of the whole of public life just begun will get and maintain deep roots."

The energized Volkskammer welcomed the government declaration and established its own committees to probe past corruption and misuse of office. On Saturday, November 18, it heard an initial report from the state prosecutor on brutality against demonstrators in East Berlin and elsewhere the previous October 7 and 8. Some seventy-six investigations were under way, it was told, that might lead to indictments of police officers and secret police officers. The same day New Forum, the group that had spearheaded those protests, held its first officially permitted meeting; 50,000 people attended.

That weekend, the second after the breaching of the wall, the East German news service ADN reported that more than 3 million East Germans had visited West Germany and West Berlin. A total of 10.3 million visas had been issued for travel to the West, and fifty new border crossings had been knocked out of the wall in Berlin and along the East-West German border. The Sunday Krenz moved out of the elite ghetto of suburban Wandlitz to a more humble Berlin apartment under the glare of television cameras. Hundreds of thousands demonstrated in various cities for an end to the communist monopoly on power and for punishment of those responsible for the country's crisis. In less than a month Mielke and two-thirds of the old Politburo would be the subjects of prosecutors' investigations. . . .

On December 1 the Volkskammer, after deliberations that lasted all of fifteen minutes, voted to strike from the constitution article 1 guaranteeing the leading role of "the working class and its Marxist-Leninist party."

As breathtaking as they were, the political changes could not reverse the GDR's tailspin. In November industrial production dropped 2.5 percent below that of the previous year. Also in November 130,000 more East Germans moved to the Federal Republic, for an interim 1989 total of 305,000. West German athletic halls, pressed into use as temporary dormitories after the regular refugee camps and Bundeswehr barracks overflowed, themselves began to spill over. Disgruntled West Germans complained about a coming unification by evacuation. Old jokes revived about instructing the penultimate person to quit the GDR to leave a note to Erich (Honecker) asking him to turn out the lights when he too left.

The Revolution Spreads

By now the note would also have to be addressed to Todor [Zhivkov], Milos [Jakes], and Nicolae [Ceausescu, communist leaders of Bulgaria, Czechoslovakia, and Romania, respectively]. Within ten days of the wall's fall, the East German revolution had leapt to Bulgaria and Czechoslovakia. Soon it would consume the Romanian despots in the one country where it turned bloody. More slowly, it would catalyze a coup in Moscow that would fail, but would accelerate the final implosion of the three-century-old Russian empire. Within ten months Germans would be united and squabbling like any old married couple. Within a year and a half Yugoslavia would be a caldron.

This was not the way the cold war was supposed to end in anybody's book. Peace activists had hoped for a preliminary improvement in human nature and a rejection of those Mephistophelian nuclear weapons, and had feared that a nuclear catastrophe might first have to sober mankind into giving up stereotypes of enemies. The left had bet on Western acceptance of Communist party rule in Eastern Europe based on a humane "third way" between Stalinist and capitalist exploitation that would be egalitarian, ecologically sound, and socialist.

Western conservatives were much closer to the mark in anticipating the rout of Marxism in Eastern Europe once the guns were removed and people discovered that democracy and a (relatively) free market constrain the human spirit far less than any other system. But in its heart of hearts, the right had not believed that the West's policy of containment of Soviet ambitions abroad really would turn the Kremlin inward to domestic reform. Even the diplomatic practitioners of containment, studiously avoiding its inflation into "rollback" after 1956, had worried that uncontrolled East European surges for freedom might upset stability and risk war. Gradualism was the order of the day. German division was deemed necessary for stability and peace. Reunification would be possible only, if at all, at the end of a long process of East-West rapprochement, after the opposing blocs had vanished. Everyone knew that the GDR would be the last to free itself from Soviet tutelage.

The Creation of the Web

by Dawn Levy

Although the Internet had existed since 1969, few realized its potential as an information and commercial tool. Only the military and a handful of academicians made use of the network in its early days. In 1990 Tim Berners-Lee, a physicist at the European Laboratory for Particle Physics (CERN), bought the computer that would become the world's first World Wide Web server. With this machine (and the protocols and software he would develop on it), Berners-Lee would go on to usher in the modern Internet age. With a colleague named Robert Cailliau, a fellow CERN physicist, Berners-Lee developed the software that would allow remote computers to link up, share, and retrieve information. Berners-Lee's World Wide Web made it possible to access information on the Internet, and when the first server went online on December 12, 1991, the world was forever changed.

The Internet has become such an indispensable business and information tool that to be without it is a heavy disadvantage. Much as the telephone morphed from a luxury to a necessity, so too has the World Wide Web. Billions of dollars' worth of business are conducted online each year, and whole libraries are now available at one's fingertips. One would be hard-pressed to name a business or organization that did not have an Internet presence, and the growth of web-based technology and business fueled the economic boom of the 1990s.

In the following essay *Stanford Report* science writer Dawn Levy traces the beginnings and the development of the World Wide Web.

The World Wide Web came to America 10 years ago today [December 12, 2001], followed by revolutions in commerce and community. "Today, if you don't have access to the web, you're considered disadvantaged," says physicist Paul Kunz, who on Dec. 12, 1991, installed the first web server in America on an IBM mainframe computer at the Stanford Linear Accelerator Center (SLAC). Kunz recounts how a project initiated to support fundamental research evolved into what is now, more or less, an archive of humanity's collective memory.

In the late 1960s, the U.S. Department of Defense sponsored research at American universities aimed at building a communications network that could survive a nuclear attack. Computers were linked through phone lines to form networks, and the research goal was to calculate the next-best path for routing packets of information if a node in the most efficient pathway were obliterated.

On Labor Day weekend of 1969, the first packets blazed a pioneering path through the packet-switching Arpanet (for Advanced Research Projects Agency Network), providing a thoroughfare for electronic mail, file transfer, remote computer access and postings to bulletin boards and newsgroups. Arpanet paved the way for other networks, such as the National Science Foundation's NSFNet. These networks collectively became known as the Internet.

Berners-Lee Opens the Floodgates

Information trickled over the Internet in its early years, as only academicians were allowed to use it. (Open commercial and public use was not allowed until the late 1980s.) In 1990, physicist-turned-programmer Tim Berners-Lee and colleague Robert Cailliau at the European Laboratory for Particle Physics (CERN) in Switzerland began to collaborate on something that eventually opened the floodgates to mass use by turning the Internet into an ocean navigable by anyone able to point and click a mouse.

"It's too easy to say that by some accident some guy in a high-energy physics lab happened to invent the web," Kunz says. "Or to say, 'Eh, collaborative work—it was something that was about to happen anyway.' If you really look at the whole history of networking, you can see that the academic research community continuously played a role in building up all the stuff that was needed for this final coup."

In September 1990 at CERN, Berners-Lee bought a NeXT computer, manufactured by the company Steve Jobs started when he left Apple. Touted as the next great thing in desktop publishing, it was desirable for two reasons. First, its underlying operating system was UNIX, and the academic community had developed UNIX with the Internet in mind. It came with a full suite of Internet protocols and could send windows of information to remote machines. Second, it featured excellent tools for building an application with a graphical user interface, which launched commands by clicking on objects instead of by entering text.

"The ease with which one could develop applications on the NeXT was remarkable," Kunz says. "Any mere mortal with a good idea could program up his application in a reasonable amount of time, try it out and see if it really worked and then show it off to others. Using the Internet to distribute the software freely, the programmer could get other people to use it."

Berners-Lee's NeXT computer would become the world's first web server. By Christmas, Berners-Lee and Cailliau had set it up to store information and transmit it upon request. They also had developed software and protocols to link information from remote computers and allow it to be located and retrieved over the Internet by programs called browsers. Berners-Lee created the first browser. Later, physicist Tony Johnson at SLAC, a national laboratory operated by Stanford University for the Department of Energy, created another important early browser, named Midas.

Hypertext Transfer Protocol

The magic wand enabling information retrieval over the Internet was a set of instructions that transmitted hypertext, the language through which computers "talk" to each other. Called hypertext transfer protocol (HTTP), it enabled electronic linkage of one part of a document to another part of the same document; the user just clicks on the link, and the screen jumps to that section. While hypertext was not a new idea, transmitting it was. Berners-Lee expanded its application to allow links to fetch documents on other computers in a network. "All he had to do to do that was add yet another protocol to the Internet," Kunz says. "But since the Internet was open, he could do that without asking anybody, without going through a central committee." The ability to transfer hypertext transformed the arcane Internet into the accessible World

Wide Web, which literally put the world at one's fingertips.

This was all well and good, but in 1990 the World Wide Web had all the reach of a hairnet. All the world's web servers were at CERN; information traveled no farther than a few buildings.

SLAC physicist and software developer Paul Kunz had no idea that he was about to make history when, on Aug. 20, 1991, he read an announcement that Berners-Lee had posted to a newsgroup for users of NeXT's operating system, NeXTStep. It told of a way to use the Internet to cross-reference and distribute documents around the world. Kunz's eyes glazed with boredom at the topic of document distribution. He recalls: "I kind of shrugged: 'What

The World Wide Web was launched in 1991, revolutionizing business and bringing forth the information age.

are these crazy CERN people up to now?' I didn't even fetch the free software to try it out." Plus he was busy preparing to leave for Sweden to give lectures on object-oriented programming.

After Sweden, Kunz took the occasion to go to Switzerland to visit CERN, where every day was a whirlwind of meetings. Finally, on Sept. 13, Kunz's last day there, Berners-Lee insisted that he visit his office for a demonstration. Kunz also had a NeXT computer, one he bought in February 1989 to create a much easier system for physics analyses. *There are so few of us in high-energy physics using these machines*, Kunz thought. *How can I say no?*

When Berners-Lee demonstrated information retrieval via the Internet between NeXT computers, Kunz was unimpressed. But when Berners-Lee showed that he could send a query to CERN's IBM mainframe computer and retrieve results based on that query, Kunz started to get interested.

Platform-independent communication opened up a world of possibilities. But could it work between computers half a world apart?

"Tim couldn't demonstrate how well this is going to work over the Internet because all the world's web servers were at CERN," Kunz says. "In fact, it could have been that all of them were in the same building. It's not a very exciting demo."

So they used the Internet to upload Kunz's computer at SLAC with the browser software. A click at CERN got the browser running at SLAC. The SLAC machine sent a request for information to a server at CERN. The CERN server sent a web page to SLAC. And the SLAC browser sent the page's window to CERN. To accomplish all this, information had to make four transatlantic crossings.

"We were both shocked at how well it worked," Kunz recalls.

Kunz and Berners-Lee discussed making available a meaty bibliographic database of 300,000 physics references called SPIRES-HEP, for Stanford Public Information Retrieval System—High Energy Physics, maintained since 1974 by SLAC librarians.

Kunz left CERN the next day and demonstrated the web to SLAC's associate head librarian, Louise Addis, and others by connecting to the only web servers that existed at that time, the CERN computers. Everyone was impressed with the speed of the connection, which was as fast as today's connections.

When Kunz asked Addis if she wanted him to install a web

server connected to the library SPIRES database, her answer was an emphatic yes. She instantly saw the value of making SLAC's substantial catalog of online documents available to physicists worldwide.

On Dec. 12, 1991, Kunz sent an e-mail to Berners-Lee asking him to try out SLAC's newly installed web server.

"Good job!" Berners-Lee e-mailed back. "Congratulations to all involved. It seems to work well."

The next month Berners-Lee demonstrated his World Wide Web application to more than 200 physicists from around the world who were meeting in Southern France. For his grand finale, he connected to the SLAC server and did a SPIRES-HEP search.

"People went home from this meeting telling their colleagues of a new way to access SPIRES-HEP," Kunz says. "It was called the World Wide Web, and it was great."

Killer Apps

At SLAC, computer systems specialist George Crane, physicist Tony Johnson, Kunz and Addis completed the work necessary to make SPIRES-HEP's deluge of data and documents instantly available. Addis coordinated what would become the first U.S. website, which featured a search interface she created. For publish-or-perish physicists, Berners-Lee has said, information retrieval from SPIRES-HEP became the web's so-called "killer app"—the application that compelled that community to start using the technology.

Other killer apps—from e-mail to eBay, Medline to Match.com, ways to share every type of information from music to stock prices—drove other communities to the web. Today the web is a global marketplace of goods and ideas, a major economic driver, a place to connect unconstrained by geography or society. A spaceship no longer has to land for us to know that we are not alone.

Academicians had no idea their networking project would change the world. Having pushed technology to the limit to meet their specific needs, they were truly amazed when the technology in turn pushed the rest of the world toward a heady future. "But that's how things blossomed," Kunz concludes. "Very low-level, fundamental protocols that we use today were invented in these earlier days as ad hoc ways of satisfying needs amongst the research community that happened to be on this network."

E
V
E
N
T

9

The Soviet Union Dissolves:
December 25, 1991

The Death of the Soviet Union Shatters the Old World Order

by the *Economist*

By the summer of 1991 communism was breathing its last breath in
Europe. The Berlin Wall had fallen and Germany was reunified.
The Warsaw Pact, the Communist answer to the North Atlantic
Treaty Organization (NATO), was dead and the Communist regimes
of its former member nations had been swept from power. Mikhail
Gorbachev, president of the Soviet Union and architect of the Soviet
reform movements known as glasnost and perestroika, was trying
desperately to keep his nation from dissolving. Gorbachev was
caught between the hard-line Communist faction of his government—which had lost considerable power and influence as a result
of Gorbachev's reforms—and the reformers who were inspired by
the wave of liberation that swept through Eastern Europe. Many of
the republics that made up the Soviet Union were clamoring for independence. The Baltic republics of Latvia, Estonia, and Lithuania
had already declared themselves independent nations, and Ukraine
was on the verge of doing the same. On August 19, 1991, a triumvi-
rate of hard-line Communist Party members consisting of Soviet
vice president Gennady Yanaev, Prime Minister Valentin Pavlov,
and Oleg Baklanov, deputy chairman of the Soviet Defense Council, all of whom were alarmed by the dismantling of the old Soviet

---

"The Post-Soviet World: The Resumption of History," *Economist*, vol. 325, December 26,
1992, p. 67. Copyright © 1992 by Economist Newspaper Ltd. Reproduced by permission.

system, placed Gorbachev under house arrest and took control of the government. In a decree issued to the public, the hard-liners claimed that Gorbachev was in poor health and no longer able to govern the nation. Tanks and troops were deployed in Moscow as a show of force by the plotters of the coup. The attempt to overthrow the government failed, however, as troops refused to fire on the reformers, who were led by Russian president Boris Yeltsin. The rebels were arrested, and Gorbachev was restored to power.

Although communism in the Soviet Union had already been dying a long, slow death, the coup hastened its end and caused the demise of the Soviet Union itself. Throughout 1991 Gorbachev had been working on a treaty that would preserve the Union and the Communist Party. He appeared to be making progress when the hard-liners tried to oust him. In the aftermath of the coup, other, more liberal leaders like Boris Yeltsin, who favored a looser confederation of states, had eclipsed Gorbachev in power and influence. When the coup plotters were arrested, Yeltsin immediately banned the Communist Party in the Russian Republic, and on December 25, 1991, Gorbachev resigned as president of the Soviet Union and officially handed power over to the Russian president. The Soviet Union was officially dead.

In the following essay the editors of the *Economist* explain how the death of the Soviet Union profoundly altered the geopolitical landscape. It immediately created fifteen new nations, and with the collapse of the Communist specter that had loomed over Europe and the rest of the world, the United States and Europe were able to devote more time to domestic issues. As a result, Western expenditures on the military were soon directed toward other purposes. The Soviet collapse also meant the death of the proxy conflicts that had been raging around the globe. The Soviets had been one of the biggest military suppliers to the Arab nations in their conflicts with Israel. The *Economist* contends that the collapse of the Soviet Union shrunk the Arab-Israeli conflict down to more manageable proportions. The demise of the Soviets also meant that the West no longer felt obligated to support right-wing regimes in the Third World. According to the *Economist*, the death of the Soviet Union has made the world a much more diverse, as well as a much more unstable, place. The *Economist* is a weekly journal that is published in six countries. It holds to the ideals of free trade, internationalism, and minimal government interference in business and personal affairs.

As a political earthquake, the end of the Soviet empire measures right at the top of the Richter scale. The first shock has created a score of new countries, toppled numerous governments and shattered the Old World Order. It has affected everything from the Olympic Games (all those new flags in Barcelona, and for once no boycotts) to defence budgets and western elections. It has given the United Nations new members and influence. And this is just the start. By the time the aftershocks are over and the dust has settled, the global landscape will look utterly different.

For these are still early post-Soviet days. The Soviet Union ended just one year ago [in 1991], even though it already seems an aeon. The consequences of events of this scale tend to take decades or more to unfold. The ramifications of the collapse of the Habsburg and Ottoman empires—not to mention the Macedonian and Roman ones—are still being played out in the Balkans.

The Soviet Union's was no ordinary empire, for two reasons. First, its power. It was large, though others (the British empire, for example) have been larger. Beyond territory, however, it was an empire of ideas, a system of thought that the rulers in Moscow sought to spread across the world. That, plus the nuclear weapons capable of projecting Soviet power anywhere, gave this empire global reach.

For a generation of third-world leaders, in particular, Soviet communism represented an alternative model of political and economic control. Even after the model began to lose its lustre, as it did well before Mikhail Gorbachev reached the Kremlin, the Soviet Union was a source of military and technical support for local powers involved in what the superpowers turned into proxy conflicts for their East-West struggle. The East-West struggle set the co-ordinates for much of what happened in the world; those co-ordinates vanished with the Soviet Union.

"A Unique Event in Human History"

The way the country vanished is the second peculiarity of the Soviet empire. "It was a unique event in human history," says Sir Isaiah Berlin, an Oxford philosopher. "Never before has there been a case of an empire that caved in without a war, revolution or an invasion." Even the implosion of the Roman empire happened with the help of attacks by barbarians. The Soviet Union simply withered away. That suggests that some unusual forces have been at work.

Indeed, so all-embracing are the potential implications of the Soviet break-up that it can be used to explain almost anything. Take Yugoslavia. War might not have broken out if the place had remained locked between the rivalry of the two superpowers. And did the end of the "evil empire" cost George Bush the American presidency? A case can be made: the absence of international threat left Americans free to concentrate on domestic issues (Mr Bush's weakness) and allowed them the luxury of voting for Ross Perot; the effect of end-of-cold-war defence cuts on California's economy may have helped to turn America's biggest state Democratic.

Even the recent chaos in West European currency markets can be traced back to the end of the Soviet empire. The high German interest rates that put such a strain on Europe's exchange-rate mechanism (ERM) were a result of the costs of absorbing East Germany; the flurry of currency speculation that led to the withdrawal from the ERM of sterling and the Italian lira started in Finland, whose economy was reeling from the shock of the collapse of the Soviet market; and so on.

Yet any such analysis ought to carry a warning: attempts to explain too many events or trends as merely fall-out from the Soviet Union's fall can seriously damage historical accuracy. In all three examples—Yugoslavia, the American election, the currency turmoil—the Soviet element is just one part of a complicated story. Later, this article will ignore all health warnings and indulge in some enjoyable speculation about, for example, the significance of the Soviet disintegration for the future of the modern state. But first it looks at what can more safely be said about the changes already brought about as a result of the Soviet drama. For that, a quick tour of the world is needed.

Around the World in Weighty Ways

Start in Asia, where the Soviet retreat from Afghanistan was the beginning of the withdrawal from empire. Now that retreat has turned into disintegration, strategic calculations in the entire region have changed drastically. In East Asia, the Americans may be starting to follow the Russian example by going home, leaving a potentially dangerous vacuum for other big regional powers—Japan, China, India—to ponder.

Japan is striving to identify the best role for itself in that Pacific vacuum; should it be the local representative of the G7, or an Asian-style military power in its own right? China took a look at the Soviet debacle and concluded that the main cause was economic; the result has been to jolt Chinese economic reform forwards. India had based its defence policy on the assumption of Soviet support, including military supplies. It cannot expect the same level of support from the new Russia, so it is turning to other countries, such as America and Israel, to fill the gap.

Pakistan, in theory a cold-war winner, in practice finds that the West needs it less and is therefore prepared to put more pressure on it—notably over its nuclear-weapons programme. Pakistan also has to worry, along with China and others, about the possibility that the break-up of ex-Soviet Central Asia will spread to their own countries, with conflict among ethnic groups and more redrawing of borders. Much will depend on the struggle for influence in Central Asia that also involves Turkey and Iran.

Our tour moves briskly on to the Middle East, where the Arab-Israeli conflict has ceased to be part of superpower politics and has thus shrunk to more manageable dimensions. Peace, for once, looks possible. The Arabs have lost their main military supplier and the prospect of superpower support against Israel in a war; that is leading some countries, such as Syria, to woo America. Israel is suffering from the "Pakistan syndrome": its enemies have been weakened, but its main friend, America, has felt freer to twist its arm—over Jewish settlements in the West Bank, for instance. One way or another, events in the ex–Soviet Union determined the result of the Israeli election [in June 1992]; Soviet emigres voted overwhelmingly for Yitzhak Rabin's Labor Party.

From Moscow to Mozambique

In Africa it is worth lingering a little longer. The Soviet fall-out has led to more changes there than anywhere else in the world except Europe, for three main reasons. 1. The demise of central planning. In the 1960s and 1970s, the Soviet model of economic development—including nationalization on a grand scale—was accepted in many parts of Africa, even in some countries which professed to be capitalist. Tanzania and Ethiopia went so far as to introduce collective farming, with disastrous consequences. African leaders studied at Soviet universities and used Marxist language to explain their policies. All this changed as the Soviet

The Former Soviet Union

model fell apart. From 1989, several African countries began converting to more market-minded philosophies; Zambia and Tanzania were examples. Across the continent, private enterprise is now being given more scope. 2. The end of Africa's proxy wars. The Soviet Union financed insurgencies and governments all over Africa. When the Soviet Union collapsed, the rulers of Angola, Mozambique and Ethiopia were no longer able to continue fighting their anti-communist rebels. The Ethiopian government fell. In Mozambique the Marxist regime began trying to negotiate peace. Angola's civil war, which was supposed to be left versus right, degenerated into tribal war. The ideological veneer had worn away.

The end of Soviet involvement in Africa also meant that the West no longer felt it had to support right-wing, pro-American regimes. Hence the change in western policies towards Africa: the reluctance to give aid without seeing any results, the pressure on various dictators to democratize. For example, pressure can be put on President Daniel arap Moi of Kenya to hold elections because Kenya is no longer seen as a bastion of anti-communism in East Africa. The same is true of Kamuzu Banda of Malawi. However, just as the fall of Soviet-backed communist rulers is not complete (witness Fidel Castro in Cuba), so the fall of America's former puppets in Africa has some way to go (witness Mobutu Sese Seko in Zaire). 3. The example of "people power".

There are too many televisions in Africa for dictators' comfort; a lot of African rulers watched the Romanian revolution with great trepidation. Their fear of suffering the same fate as the Ceausescus has been another reason for the wave of democratisation in Africa.

All three of those influences apply in South Africa. For years, the official ideology in South Africa was as much anti-communist as racist. The government always claimed to be fighting the African National Congress (ANC) because it was backed by the Soviet Union (which indeed it was) and believed in central planning, not merely because it was black. When it no longer made any sense to go on seeing the ANC as a terrorist organization controlled by the Kremlin, and when South Africa's rulers realised that they were no longer under threat from Soviet-backed regimes in Angola and Mozambique, negotiation became possible. Both the ANC and the government also took note of "people power". One faction within the ANC advocates using it to unseat the government; the fear of mass unrest is a further incentive for whites to search for a political settlement.

Back to the Centre

And so to Europe, the heart of the upheaval. The continent is transformed:

New countries. A look at the map shows the extent of change. A clutch of new countries has appeared out of the old Soviet Union. Two Germanies have become one. Czechoslovakia and Yugoslavia have split up.

New politics. Across Eastern Europe, new regimes have come to power, most with at least a superficial commitment to democracy. In many places, though, nationalism is rampant. Xenophobic nationalism is also on the rise in some West European countries, partly in response to the growing numbers of refugees from the ex-communist East. West European politics has been affected in other ways, too. Communist parties have been losing votes, despite name-changes and other attempts to move with the times. In Italy, which had the largest communist party in Western Europe, this is playing havoc with the post-1945 balance of power.

New economics. The post-communist governments in Eastern Europe are all replacing central planning with the market, albeit at varying speeds and with differing degrees of enthusiasm. The biggest privatization drive in history is under way. In the long run this should spur growth. But the cost of transition is proving high. Most of Eastern Europe is suffering from slump, with rapidly rising unemployment, high (in places hyper-) inflation and a collapse of markets in the now-disbanded Comecon trading block. The eastern slump is hurting Western Europe too—above all through the high German interest rates caused by the cost of salvaging eastern Germany.

New powers. Germany, Turkey and Ukraine stand out as countries with greatly enhanced influence in post-Soviet Europe. Germany's new-found weight is obvious. It is bigger, and suddenly has opportunities to its east; in time, as it overcomes its unification burdens, it may start throwing its weight about. Turkey also finds itself with suddenly expanded horizons, especially in Turkic-speaking parts of the Trans-caucasus and ex-Soviet Central Asia; it has the chance to become the champion of the secular model of development for Islamic countries. Ukraine, meanwhile, is a big new force in Eastern Europe: a place the size of France, between Poland and Russia, with a large (and for the moment nuclear-armed) army.

New European disorder. As the Soviet empire crumbled, so did the post-second-world-war order arranged at Yalta and Potsdam. It has been replaced by a plethora of uncertainties. America's military presence in Europe—indeed the long-term future of the Atlantic alliance—can no longer be taken for granted; already the number of American servicemen there is set to shrink well below 150,000, from 330,000 in 1989. The ex–Warsaw Pact countries of east-central Europe are in a security limbo. Now that they no longer sit between competing power-blocks, neutral countries—Finland, Sweden, Austria, even Switzerland—are having to reconsider the concept of neutrality. One of the neutrals, Yugoslavia, has imploded; others are rushing for the supposed safety of the European Community.

But the Community is itself in turmoil. It too was a child of the post-war order: a club of West European states which tended to refer to themselves as "Europe", as if the eastern half of the continent did not exist. The treaty signed [in 1991] in the Dutch city of Maastricht was in part a panicky response to events in the East, an attempt by the club to press ahead with its own agenda of closer integration before it was too late, keeping Germany contained and even (as French ministers explained) turning "Europe" into a match for the sole remaining superpower, America.

The troubles that have since plagued the Maastricht treaty suggest that the attempt may have been misguided. The fall of the Soviet empire is pushing forward a different agenda, top of which is the question of the Community's enlargement to include new members.

Guess What?

All that amounts to a formidable catalogue of change. But the Soviet disunion may in time be seen to have even bigger consequences. It may be the trigger of trends that are still only dimly discernible, if at all. Here are four guesses.

The end of the West? "The East", as a geopolitical concept, is obsolete; it was a synonym for the Soviet empire. Where does that leave "the West", which defined itself largely by contrast with "the East" (hence Japan's commonly accorded status as a "western" country)? Perhaps NATO will survive. Even if it does not, something like "the West" may well endure as a group of countries with common basic values. Maybe, speculates Helmut Sonnenfeldt of the Brookings Institution in Washington, this group will also remain bound together by a sense of external threat—fear of chaos or Islamic extremism, say, from "the South" rather than the East. Nevertheless, the West is likely to become a looser, more argumentative grouping.

The end of superpowerdom? It has become commonplace to talk of America as the sole remaining superpower. But it is possible that the fall of the Soviet Union will come to show that superpower status is not sustainable. In "The Rise and Fall of the Great Powers", Paul Kennedy argued that a country's might in the end depends on the strength of its economic base, and that the balance of global productive forces has been shifting towards countries such as China and Japan. Even in purely military terms, the old bipolar dominance of America and the Soviet Union (or now Russia) is shrinking as they reduce their nuclear arsenals while lesser nuclear powers (Britain, France, China) retain plans to increase theirs and new countries set about joining the nuclear club. The Soviet break-up could hasten the spread of nuclear know-how and hardware.

The end of the modern state? Economic failure was not the only reason for the Soviet disintegration. Ethnic fission also played its part. "Splittism" has spread to many sub-regions of the former Soviet Union (such as Checheno-Ingushetia and Transdniestria), as well as to Yugoslavia and Czechoslovakia—not to mention places like Belgium and Canada. "It is not inevitable that the nation-state will last," concludes Francois Heisbourg, one of France's brightest strategic thinkers.

Mr Heisbourg also points out that the whole system that evolved in the 16th and 17th centuries, of the nation-state and its absolute sovereignty, is being threatened. Sovereignty is being eroded by technology and the growing power of supranational bodies such as the United Nations and the European Community. The force of nationalism may mean that ever smaller ethnic groups become the prime unit in which people organize themselves. Sir Ralf Dahrendorf, warden of St Antony's College in Oxford, believes one lesson of the Soviet collapse is that dictatorial power can no longer hold multi-national countries together.

The Resumption of History

The end of history? Certainly not. To be fair to Francis Fukuyama, the champion of the idea, he may be right that liberal democracy continues to triumph around the world. On the other hand, he may not. Rival ideologies—based on race, religion, or whatever—could yet challenge it. Democracy in much of Eastern Europe is fragile, and threatened by the strains of the transition to a market economy and the darker political forces ready to exploit them. John Gray, a political theorist at Oxford University, predicts that Eastern Europe's period of democratic institutions will be short-lived.

It is still too early to tell whether the benefits from the fall of the Soviet empire will outweigh the costs. The benefits could, with luck, include a huge advance in freedom and prosperity. With bad luck, the costs could include a huge increase in local conflict and in the numbers of countries with nuclear weapons. Either way, the end of the Soviet empire makes the world a more diverse, more unstable, more unpredictable place. It marks the resumption of history.

Mikhail Gorbachev's Resignation Speech

by Mikhail Gorbachev

The following is the resignation speech delivered by Soviet Union president Mikhail Gorbachev on December 25, 1991. In this speech Gorbachev discusses the dire circumstances the Soviet Union faced when he came to power in 1985 and his efforts to reform the government and the Communist Party. He also expresses his regret concerning the splintering of the country and his hope for the future. Gorbachev had hoped that the Soviet Union might survive as a federal entity, and he appeared to be making progress toward that goal through intense negotiations. The coup of August 19, 1991, put an end to that possibility, however; more liberal leaders like Boris Yeltsin, who supported only a very loose confederation of independent republics, gained significant political influence. When Gorbachev stepped down and handed power over to Yeltsin, the Soviet Union ceased to exist.

 ear fellow countrymen, compatriots. Due to the situation which has evolved as a result of the formation of the Commonwealth of Independent States, I hereby discon-

---

Mikhail Gorbachev, resignation speech, December 25, 1991.

tinue my activities at the post of President of the Union of Soviet Socialist Republics.

I am making this decision on considerations of principle. I firmly came out in favor of the independence of nations and sovereignty for the republics. At the same time, I support the preservation of the union state and the integrity of this country.

The developments took a different course. The policy prevailed of dismembering this country and disuniting the state which is something I cannot subscribe to.

After the Alma-Ata meeting [a 1991 meeting during which the fate of the Soviet Union was decided] and its decisions, my position did not change as far as this issue is concerned. Besides, it is my conviction that decisions of this caliber should have been made on the basis of popular will.

However, I will do all I can to insure that the agreements that were signed there lead toward real concord in society and facilitate the exit out of this crisis and the process of reform.

This being my last opportunity to address you as President of the U.S.S.R., I find it necessary to inform you of what I think of the road that has been trodden by us since 1985.

I find it important because there have been a lot of controversial, superficial, and unbiased judgments made on this score. Destiny so ruled that when I found myself at the helm of this state it already was clear that something was wrong in this country.

We had a lot of everything—land, oil and gas, other natural resources—and there was intellect and talent in abundance. However, we were living much worse than people in the industrialized countries were living and we were increasingly lagging behind them. The reason was obvious even then. This country was suffocating in the shackles of the bureaucratic command system. Doomed to cater to ideology, and suffer and carry the onerous burden of the arms race, it found itself at the breaking point.

All the half-hearted reforms—and there have been a lot of them—fell through, one after another. This country was going nowhere and we couldn't possibly live the way we did. We had to change everything radically.

It is for this reason that I have never had any regrets—never had any regrets—that I did not use the capacity of General Secretary just to reign in this country for several years. I would have considered it an irresponsible and immoral decision. I was also aware that to embark on reform of this caliber and in a society like ours was an extremely difficult and even risky undertaking. But even now, I am convinced that the democratic reform that we launched in the spring of 1985 was historically correct.

The process of renovating this country and bringing about drastic change in the international community has proven to be much more complicated than anyone could imagine. However let us give its due to what has been done so far.

This society has acquired freedom. It has been freed politically and spiritually, and this is the most important achievement that we have yet fully come to grips with. And we haven't, because we haven't learned to use freedom yet.

However, an effort of historical importance has been carried out. The totalitarian system has been eliminated, which prevented this country from becoming a prosperous and well-to-do country a long time ago. A breakthrough has been effected on the road of democratic change.

Free elections have become a reality. Free press, freedom of worship, representative legislatures and a multi-party system have all become reality. Human rights are being treated as the supreme principle and top priority Movement has been started toward a multi-tier economy and the equality of all forms of ownership is being established.

Within the framework of the land reform, peasantry began to reemerge as a class. And there arrived farmers, and billions of hectares of land are being given to urbanites and rural residents alike. The economic freedom of the producer has been made a law, and free enterprise, the emergence of joint stock companies and privatization are gaining momentum.

As the economy is being steered toward the market format, it is important to remember that the intention behind this reform is the well-being of man, and during this difficult period everything should be done to provide for social security, which particularly concerns old people and children.

We're now living in a new world. An end has been put to the cold war and to the arms race, as well as to the mad militarization of the country, which has crippled our economy, public attitudes and morals. The threat of nuclear war has been removed.

Once again, I would like to stress that during this transitional period, I did everything that needed to be done to insure that there was reliable control of nuclear weapons. We opened up ourselves to the rest of the world, abandoned the practices of interfering in others' internal affairs and using troops outside this country, and we were reciprocated with trust, solidarity, and respect.

We have become one of the key strongholds in terms of restructuring modern civilization on a peaceful democratic basis. The nations and peoples of this country have acquired the right to freely choose their format for self-determination. Their search for democratic reform of this multinational state had led us to the point where we were about to sign a new union treaty.

All this change had taken a lot of strain and took place in the context of fierce struggle against the background of increasing resistance by the reactionary forces, both the party and state structures and the economic elite, as well as our habits, ideological bias, the sponging attitudes.

The change ran up against our intolerance, a low level of political culture and fear of change. That is why we have wasted so much time. The old system fell apart even before the new system began to work. Crisis of society as a result aggravated even further.

I'm aware that there is popular resentment as a result of today's grave situation. I note that authority at all levels, and myself are being subject to harsh criticisms. I would like to stress once again, though, that the cardinal change in so vast a country, given its heritage, could not have been carried out without difficulties, shock and pain.

The August coup brought the overall crisis to the limit. The most dangerous thing about this crisis is the collapse of statehood. I am concerned about the fact that the people in this country are ceasing to become citizens of a great power and the consequences may be very difficult for all of us to deal with.

I consider it vitally important to preserve the democratic achievements which have been attained in the last few years. We have paid with all our history and tragic experience for these democratic achievements, and they are not to be abandoned, whatever the circumstances, and whatever the pretexts. Otherwise, all our hopes for the best will be buried. I am telling you all this honestly and straightforwardly because this is my moral duty.

I would like to express my gratitude to all people who have given their support to the policy of renovating this country and became involved in the democratic reform in this country. I am also thankful to the statements, politicians and public figures, as well as millions of ordinary people abroad who understood our intentions, gave their support and met us halfway. I thank them for their sincere cooperation with us.

I am very much concerned as I am leaving this post. However, I also have feelings of hope and faith in you, your wisdom and force of spirit. We are heirs of a great civilization and it now depends on all and everyone whether or not this civilization will make a comeback to a new and decent living today. I would like, from the bottom of my heart, to thank everyone who has stood by me throughout these years, working for the righteous and good cause.

Of course, there were mistakes made that could have been avoided, and many of the things that we did could have been done better. But I am positive that sooner or later, some day our common efforts will bear fruit and our nations will live in a prosperous, democratic society.

I wish everyone all the best.

South Africa Holds Its First Multiracial
Elections: April 29, 1994

The Election Marks the Birth of Genuine Democracy in South Africa

by *Commonweal*

From 1948 to the early 1990s, apartheid was the official social policy of South Africa. Under this system of legal segregation, blacks
were barred from politics and land ownership and were denied the
right to choose where to live, work, or go to school. Throughout the
1980s, international protest against apartheid intensified, with many
nations refusing to do business with South African companies and
boycotting their products. In 1990, in response to such pressure as
well as to internal opposition, South African president F.W. de
Klerk began to relax the nation's policies. He legalized the country's main opposition group, the African National Congress (ANC),
and released its popular leader, Nelson Mandela, from prison. He
also promised to create a new constitution that granted political
power to the nation's blacks. By the end of 1991, all apartheid laws
had been eliminated, and de Klerk and Mandela had begun working
out a new system of government. In 1993, de Klerk and Mandela
were awarded the Nobel Prize for their efforts at peace. In April

"A Shining Moment," *Commonweal*, vol. 121, May 20, 1994, p. 3. Copyright © 1994 by Commonweal Publishing Co., Inc. Reproduced by permission.

1994, the nation held its first multiracial elections, and Nelson Mandela was elected president.

The following selection, an editorial by the editors of *Commonweal* magazine, was written in May 1994, one month after Mandela's election. The editors describe the election of 1994 as a major step forward in the movement for true democracy in South Africa. *Commonweal* is an independent journal of opinion edited and managed by lay Catholics.

The revolution that ended forty-five years of apartheid in South Africa last month—complete with universal suffrage, new flag and national anthem ("Nkosi Sikelel iAfrika," "God Bless Africa")—was not a velvet revolution[1] a la Eastern Europe. But like the collapse of communism in 1989, it was an achievement of the highest order and a triumph of the human spirit. The courage and dignity of those voting for the first time offered a lesson for a world beleaguered by ethnic wars, religious controversies, and single-party rule. True, the legacy of apartheid, built on three hundred years of colonialist subjugation in South Africa, will not be expunged soon, if ever. But South Africa gives hope that even in the most intractable of circumstances, new beginnings can be made when there is the will and the wisdom.

Pressure and Accommodation

South Africa arrived at this moment because of the remarkable leadership of Nelson Mandela, "a leader of enormous stature, a man of firm principle and generous spirit, and a better politician than any had hoped for" *(Economist)*. It did so because of the political change of heart fostered in white South Africans by the ruling National party leader, F.W. de Klerk, and by those white liberals who fought for the repeal of apartheid from the day of its imposition. But the changes in South Africa happened in no small measure because of moral pressures exerted from abroad. At a time when Randall Robinson of TransAfrica Forum has been fasting to bring the attention of Americans to the fate of Haitians, it should be remembered that the sanctions and boycotts advocated by Robinson and others against South Africa helped create the

1. The 1989 overthrow of the Communist government of Czechoslovakia is referred to as the "velvet revolution" because it was relatively nonviolent.

critical opening that Mandela and de Klerk navigated so effectively. It was international sanctions that gradually helped to convince the dead souls in Pretoria's government that majority rule in South Africa was the country's only hope for a future.

The revolutionary changes now legally under way in South Africa were born of the blood of martyrs. Plentiful though such blood was, it alone does not account for the historic change we are witnessing. That change was achieved through painstaking organizing at the grass roots and around the world. The real miracle of last month's plebiscite was not that it was peaceful, but that it took place at all.

April's election happened because of a series of timely accommodations by all the parties concerned, brokered at critical points over the past four years since Mandela's release from prison in 1990. Credit goes to de Klerk for releasing Mandela, and for correctly gauging that the fall of the Berlin Wall [in 1989] opened new possibilities for change in South Africa. With the end of the cold war, de Klerk reasoned, the world would be looking ever more closely at South Africa and bringing pressure to bear on it. But the African National Congress (ANC) and its Communist allies would have to adjust as well to a post-communist world where the failure of command economies had become apparent to all. De Klerk was not disappointed: Mandela and the ANC quickly made room for free markets where before only nationalization would do.

Wishing to avoid a repeat of the white flight and the incitement of tribal rivalries that have destroyed much of postcolonial Africa, the ANC made other critical political concessions to guarantee that the new South Africa would not be a land only for the black majority. "To be dismissive of opposition," Mandela told a TV audience recently, "that is what was done in Angola and Mozambique. We must not make that mistake." Thus while the ANC insisted on one-person-one vote, it agreed to a five-year government of national unity that will be representative of all voting constituencies in South Africa. Rather than a winner-take-all setup, the ANC concurred that any party with 5 percent of the vote would be granted a cabinet position, as well as guaranteed seats in the new parliament. And on the local level, the ANC signed onto an agreement that residents of existing white, Indian, and colored areas would elect a minimum of at least 30 percent of local representatives.

To induce the Zulu-led Inkata Freedom Party (IFP) of Mangosuthu G. Buthelezi to participate, in February the ANC agreed to a double ballot in the elections: one for national office, the other for nine regional elections. While Chief Buthelezi held off on participating in the electoral process until a week before the plebiscite, it was the ANC's concession that weakened IFP resistance to participation. Finally, when the election itself proved poorly administered and too slow in many Inkata areas, the voting was extended a day.

This is in no way to forget that 13,000 people died in partisan political violence in South Africa since the ANC was legalized in 1990. Nor is it to say that future cooperation will be the rule in South Africa. The new government faces immediate problems of immense size and complexity: The unemployment rate of the African population is nearly 50 percent; 53 percent live below the poverty level, compared to 2 percent of whites; whites have a personal per capita income 9.5 times that of Africans; over generations, tribal violence was fanned by deliberate government policies; and white racism remains deeply entrenched.

But if gestures carry significance, perhaps one will stand out in the years ahead, a gesture candidate Mandela made to de Klerk during a debate in April [1994]. After strongly criticizing de Klerk throughout the debate, Mandela reached over to his opponent, took him by both hands, and said: "My criticism of Mr. de Klerk should not obscure one fact. We are a shining example of people drawn from different race groups who have a common loyalty, a common love for their common country."

The shining example of a South Africa that has made peace with itself while maintaining its diversity would be a timely gift for all of Africa. Mandela has pointed out that all of southern Africa was the victim of South African apartheid. South Africa's military adventures left 2 million dead and an estimated $62 billion of damage for its neighbors. Its exports of arms fueled tragedies abroad, including those of today: In 1992 South Africa sold an estimated $6 million in light arms to Rwanda.

The birth of a genuine, multiracial democracy in South Africa—one that fosters the well-being of all its peoples, particularly apartheid's most aggrieved victims—is the most important development in Africa in the last quarter of a century. It is a process we should foster with our money, our creative energies, and our prayers.

11 Israeli Prime Minister Yitzhak Rabin Is Assassinated: November 4, 1995

Rabin's Assassination Ruins a Landmark Chance for Peace

by Michael Karpin and Ina Friedman

In 1993, partly as a result of a violent six-year uprising by Palestinians in Israeli-occupied territories, Israeli prime minister Yitzhak Rabin signed the Oslo Accords. The chief stipulations of this agreement were Israeli recognition of the Palestinian Liberation Organization (PLO) and withdrawal of Israeli forces from the Gaza Strip and Jericho, both of which proved to be incredibly unpopular amongst many Israelis. While the rest of the world applauded Rabin for his efforts to bring peace to the Middle East, the prime minister faced increasingly harsh criticism and growing resistance to the peace agreement in his own country. Militant right-wing activists, religious leaders, and politicians in Israel demonized Rabin, painting him as a traitor and a Nazi who was willing to sacrifice Israeli security to placate the Arabs. On November 4, 1995, Yigal Amir, a militant Jewish law student, shot and killed Yitzhak Rabin at a peace rally in Tel Aviv.

In the following essay Michael Karpin and Ina Friedman describe how the militant views of Rabin's political foes may have directly caused his death—and the death of the peace process as well. They accuse Rabin's adversaries of orchestrating an intense smear campaign, in which thinly veiled threats of assassination were made

Michael Karpin and Ina Friedman, *Murder in the Name of God: The Plot to Kill Yitzhak Rabin*. New York: Metropolitan Books, 1998. Copyright © 1998 by Michael Karpin and Ina Friedman. Reproduced by permission of Henry Holt and Company, LLC.

and endorsed. Karpin and Friedman contend that the atmosphere created by this campaign inspired Amir to kill Rabin. The authors also argue that Rabin's assassination was an attempt to stall the peace process. Shortly after Rabin's assassination, a right-wing government came to power in Israel and immediately began to undo the Oslo agreements. Tensions between Israel and the PLO flared up again, and in September 2000 another uprising—or *Intifada*—occurred, further dimming hopes of a settlement between Israelis and Palestinians.

Michael Karpin is one of Israel's leading journalists and is editor and anchor of *Second Look*, an Israeli newsmagazine. Ina Friedman is a journalist, interpreter, and correspondent of the Dutch daily *Trouw.*

N o one can say how momentous the assassination of Yitzhak Rabin will prove to be for Israel's future. Nor is it possible to know today whether the change of course Rabin introduced will prove any more than a brief deviation from a national policy long colored by suspicion, pessimism, and ideological rigidity. What does seem certain, however, is that historians will view this period as a complex and nuanced story of a society that turned against itself and, when it had the opportunity to move from tragedy to catharsis, fled from that prospect with all possible speed.

One explanation for that flight has been offered by an astute observer of the Israeli scene, U.S. Assistant Secretary of State Martin Indyk. Upon ending his tour as U.S. ambassador to Israel in September 1997, Indyk referred in a *Ha'aretz* interview to the frenetic pace of Israeli life. "I have the feeling that part of the energy with whose aid you move from crisis to crisis, part of the rhetoric with which it is done, derives from a desire to escape from a situation that is too brutal," he observed. "I think this is also true of the Rabin assassination. The country bounced back too quickly and moved on to the next crisis, and thus it lacked the ability to truly cope, to digest what happened."

Repressing the Assassination

Indyk saw and diplomatically phrased what many Israelis are loath to admit: that rather than address and assimilate, reflect and rehabilitate, they chose to repress the Rabin assassination and treat any serious examination of the affair almost as a national taboo. Safely protected from the light of scrutiny were the individuals, parties, and organizations that had organized and funded the incitement against Rabin; the rabbis who had ruled on *din moser* [the duty to eliminate a Jew who intends to turn another Jew into non-Jewish authorities] and *din rodef* [the sentence pronounced on a Jewish traitor]; the national figures who had made thinly veiled references to the fate due a "traitor," "Nazi," and "collaborator"; the extremists who had called for discarding the democratic way of life; and the leaders of the moderate right who had allowed radical elements to dictate their program of action. Fateful questions were buried together with the body of the slain leader. The assassination was erased from the public agenda so quickly that the processes of conciliation and reform never had a chance to begin.

Before Yitzhak Rabin had even been laid to rest, the Israeli right began complaining that it was the object of a cynical campaign to lay responsibility for the violence at its doorstep. Its indignation soon spawned a spate of popular conspiracy theories that blamed Rabin for his own death. The left, consumed by shame over its complacency and failure to protect and defend Rabin prior to the assassination, fought back by portraying itself, rather than Israeli society and democracy, as the injured party. And both sides felt that an honest examination of their behavior would only aggravate the divisions within Israeli society and should thus be carefully avoided.

Indeed, hardly had the week of national mourning ended when the imperative of "national unity" was raised as a supreme value. It quickly became clear, however, that the assassination of the prime minister was not an event around which such unity could coalesce. For the dictates of solidarity would require Israelis to penetrate dark corners of religion and politics, basic halachic [Jewish religious law] issues, the relationship between religion and state, and the country's commitment to the core value of democratic rule. Paradoxically, Rabin's murder confronted them with questions deemed far more menacing and potentially divisive than any policy he had promoted during his life.

Avoidance of these questions was initially chosen by Shimon Peres as the best way to preserve the peace process, and in this case his decision was right. In the weeks following the assassination, he managed to withdraw Israeli troops from six Palestinian cities in the West Bank without any protest from the opposition. It was embraced by Benjamin Netanyahu as the means for distancing himself from his own connection to the incitement. Both camps prescribed it as the solution for healing the national rift. But it has merely allowed them to cling more tenaciously to their opposing positions.

"We Have Learned Nothing"

There was a brief moment of respite. In his postelection victory speech in June 1996 Prime Minister Netanyahu pledged to be the prime minister of all the people of Israel. A year and a half later, however, a radio microphone picked up his voice whispering into the ear of an influential Sephardi mystic: "The leftists have forgotten what it is to be Jewish." Little wonder, then, that by the second anniversary of the assassination, the incessant friction and use of the tragedy as a political weapon brought the historian Professor Shlomo Ben-Ami, a Moroccan-born immigrant who grew up in the northern development town of Kiryat Shmonah and is today the leading intellectual in Israel's Labor Party, to describe the gravity of the crisis in writing:

> The ties that hold Israel together as a united society have long been in a tragic process of disintegration. What we have here is not a society but cells inimical to one another in a state of potential civil war. Israel will not be able to stand this way before an enemy or confront the difficult challenges of peace. . . . Two years after the assassination we have learned nothing and forgotten nothing; we are in exactly the same place. This nation is not even capable of mourning together.

It will be argued, and justly so, that Israel was no less factious under Rabin's tutelage. But even as its people clashed over the course of the peace process, the country as a whole was reaping its benefits. After the Oslo Agreements Israel emerged from the diplomatic isolation of the 1980s to find itself crowded with official visitors from the Americas, the European Union, the [Commonwealth of Independent States], the Far East, and the Arab world. Israeli businesspeople plied the routes between Tel Aviv and Egypt, Jordan, North Africa, and the Persian Gulf, developing new markets as the walls of the Arab boycott crumbled and Arab regimes established diplomatic ties with Israel. Foreign investments poured into the country as the future technological and financial hub of a "new Middle East," bringing the national growth rate to 5 to 6 percent per annum. Israelis even began to fear for the ecological health of their country were it to become a crossroads of heavy commercial traffic.

Two years after the "national camp" narrowly won the 1996 election, little of this picture remained. The peace process was stalled, and the Oslo Agreements were frozen. Negotiations with Syria had not been renewed, and the Arab world had severely curtailed its contacts with Israel. The growth rate had fallen to 1 to 2 percent, and the optimism that was to have launched a thriving Israel into the twenty-first century had evaporated, casting the economy into a deep recession. The country had slid back into a "Fortress Israel" mind-set, shunned by the Arab states, at loggerheads with the European Union, and bickering with its staunchest ally, the United States, over the administration's resolve to keep the peace process alive.

A Time of Deep Anxiety

On the domestic scene no consensus had been reached by the broad political center to isolate the extremists. At the same time the violence perpetrated against the nation's leader seemed to have become infectious, as the rates of murder and domestic violence rose markedly in the intervening years. Tempers were shorter than ever; life in Israel was less tranquil (if it could ever have been described as such). Practically every sector of society, from religious and political groups to new immigrants, women, and Arabs, complained of a lack of tolerance. Antigovernment incitement continued as well, especially whenever the prospect of a further withdrawal from the territories returned to the headlines.

Historians are likely to characterize the post-Rabin period as a time of deep anxiety. There are many indications that racist and separatist philosophies are gaining ground, especially among the *haredim* [ultra-Orthodox Jews] and national religious population. One particularly troubling development is the recent waves of verbal assaults on the High Court of Justice by religious circles of both tendencies. Threats [have been] made against Chief Justice Aharon Barak. In May 1997 a crowd of *haredi* protesters rushed the Supreme Court building on the day it was hearing arguments, inter alia, against a decision to indict a leading *haredi* politician. Knesset member Aharon Cohen of the ultra-Orthodox Shas Party, which in the past decade has grown from a marginal political force to a major power, characterized the court's justices as "foreign priests of modern, primitive idolatry." Shas's spiritual mentor, former Sephardi Chief Rabbi Ovadiah Yosef, went a step further in urging all Israelis to boycott the secular courts, "which are not for Jews," and agree to be judged only before rabbinical tribunals.

A Halachic Revival

The desire to reconstitute Israel as a halachic state has also enjoyed a highly public revival since the 1996 election, in which the three religious parties won a total of twenty-three Knesset seats. The unsettling result is that over a fifth of Israel's legislature advocates a philosophy that would effectively strip the Knesset of authority. [During 1997] the uproar over an amendment that would formally recognize only those religious conversions performed in Israel by Orthodox rabbis has drawn the greatest coverage, primarily because of the intense antagonism it has sparked among the majority Conservative and Reform streams of Judaism in the United States. But within Israel itself the creeping legitimization of a halachic state is the more alarming phenomenon because of the stature of the people now promoting it.

One of them is Rabbi Yitzhak Levy, who became chairman of the National Religious Party (NRP) at the beginning of 1998 after the death of Zevulun Hammer. As minister of transport in Netanyahu's government, the soft-spoken Levy, who represents the far-right position within the NRP, made his first official visit as a cabinet minister to the yeshiva at Joseph's Tomb in Nablus and the settlement of Bracha to encourage the zealots who study or live there. In November 1997 he told an interviewer from *Ha'aretz* that he too sides with the notion of Israel's becoming a state ruled by the halacha (provided this change comes about by consensus). He does not see a conflict between a halachic state and a democratic one, he added, because the ancient law provides sufficient protection of individual rights. This view, which fifty years ago was confined to the margins of the body politic, is now being advocated at the very heart of the political establishment. Today Rabbi Levy is Israel's minister of education and culture. His colleague Hanan Porat is also strategically placed as chairman of the Knesset Constitution, Law, and Justice Committee, with considerable influence over the fate of civil rights legislation.

A Resurgence of Militant Organizations

Yet another barometer of Israeli ambivalence about the health of its democracy and the rule of law is the fact that the fanatic groups that were active in the incitement campaign against Prime Minister Rabin continue to thrive. Kach and Kahane Chai [militant Jewish organizations], which were outlawed by the Rabin government after the massacre in the Cave of the Patriarchs [on February 25, 1994, Dr. Baruch Goldstein gunned down twenty-nine Palestinians at morning prayer], pursue their activities under new names. Both have found a home in the Yeshiva of the Jewish Idea in Jerusalem. Most of the hard core of Kahane Chai is concentrated in the Samarian settlement of Tapuach and publishes a weekly newsletter, the *Way of the Torah*, that is circulated in synagogues and from distribution points at heavily frequented sites, such as the Mahane Yehudah open market in Jerusalem. Since Rabin's assassination Kahane Chai has framed its messages more gingerly. But each time there are rumors of possible movement in the peace process, threats against the government, and specifically against Netanyahu, reappear in its publications, usually under the guise of verses from the Bible.

To circumvent the ban on the two organizations, in November 1996 some of their members joined forces in establishing a new group called the Ideological Front. Four hundred people showed up for its founding meeting. They included Itamar Ben-Gvir, who tore the Cadillac symbol off Rabin's car and threatened to "get to" the prime minister as well; Natan Levy, who was one of Avishai Raviv's deputies in Eyal; Rabbi Yitzhak Ginzburg of the yeshiva in Joseph's Tomb; and Shmuel Sackett of Zo Artzenu [a militant Jewish organization]. A few of the group's leaders were subsequently interrogated by the police in connection with an attack on senior officials of the Palestinian Authority. Similar sources were suspected of being behind the death threat made against the Irish singer Sinead O'Connor, who consequently canceled a concert in Jerusalem on behalf of the Jerusalem Link, a joint Palestinian-Israeli women's peace group. Ben-Gvir publicly boasted that he had scared the singer away.

Avigdor Eskin, who pronounced the *Pulsa da-Nura* curse on Rabin, continues his provocative activities. Along with a handful of followers, Eskin has introduced a new custom by annually celebrating Yigal Amir's birthday, replete with champagne, outside the prison where the assassin is serving his life sentence. A

Beersheba taxi driver who dared protest the celebration was badly beaten by Eskin.

The Action Headquarters also continues to exist, with Ya'akov Novick on constant alert to take on the Netanyahu government if and when it votes to cede additional territory under the provisions of the Oslo Agreement. Novick's friend Baruch Marzel is as influential as ever in Hebron, where tensions periodically explode into violence and the latest strategy of the Jewish settlers is to prod Israeli troops to enter the Palestinian sector of the city, thereby wrecking the withdrawal agreement signed by Netanyahu. And Elyakim Ha'etzni of Kiryat Arba who compared Rabin to Marshal Pétain [the French leader who surrendered to the Nazis], has now trained his sights on Netanyahu and reached beyond French history all the way back to the Talmud in warning in a *Yediot Ahronot* interview:

> If Netanyahu, heaven forfend, turns over responsibility for areas of Judea and Samaria to Arafat . . . it can be expected, by simple logic, that what happened to Rabin and Peres will happen to him as well. If the Land of Israel is lost, we will fight him as we did his predecessor. In the Talmud [it is written that] an ox that has gored three times must be put to death. The Likud gored in Camp David and in Madrid, and if it gores in Oslo, then it must be put to death.

The Line Between Free Speech and Incitement

Given the experience of November 1995, should rhetoric of this sort be defined as incitement to murder? Well after the assassination some leaders of the opposition, who were by then back in power, felt secure enough to admit that criticism of the Rabin government had been stretched beyond the limit of what is permissible in a democratic society. But the Israeli legislature and legal system were still reluctant to define the line separating the exercise of free speech from the practice of illegal incitement. Before the Rabin assassination the law enforcement authorities had approached this matter with caution and restraint for fear of trampling on the cardinal right of democratic protest. Attorney General Michael Ben-Ya'ir had also advanced the pragmatic argument that trying offenders for incitement would only provide them with a platform for disseminating their views to an ever-wider audience. Immediately after the murder, stung by criticism that they had been too lenient with offenders and had misjudged the powerful influence of fanatics, the authorities initially overreacted and went to the opposite extreme. In one case a settler from the Hebron area who expressed his satisfaction over the assassination to foreign news networks was arrested and remanded for a week without bail. The newfound zeal was at any rate short-lived.

Since then some jurists and legislators have moved to amend the law and draw a clearer distinction between the right of free speech and its abuse. They propose to define incitement and sedition as explicit calls to engage in violence or perpetrate crimes against the regime, as the creation of a climate conducive to such crimes, and as defiance of the democratic and legal order. Obviously, criticism of the government or passive resistance to its policies would not be categorized as crimes, as the motivation behind new legislation is to protect the democratic system, not debase it.

One advocate of such an amendment is the Hebrew University law professor Mordechai Kremnitzer. Known for his liberal outlook, Kremnitzer nevertheless believes that in times of emergency, as when the democratic system itself is under assault, society is entitled to place constraints on freedom of speech. In various articles he has expressed deep concern over the stability of democratic rule in Israel, explaining that:

> Yitzhak Rabin was murdered because of the weakness of Israeli democracy, because of the delegitimization of the government he headed and the political line he advanced. I am not speaking of criticism, which is the life breath of democracy, but of the denial of legitimacy, whence the distance to political murder is short. . . .
> Not only did the assassination expose the weakness of Israeli democracy, it considerably enervated [that democracy], and the support for the murder and the murderer, which is hardly marginal, continues to weaken it. Israeli democracy today is not something to be taken for granted; it is frail.

Consequences

Contrary to initial expectations, then, the short-term effect of Yitzhak Rabin's assassination has been a rise in violence, rather than a sober reconsideration of its efficacy. It has also generated a decline in national self-confidence. Israelis recurrently express the fear that their country will ignite in civil war—a specter that weighs more heavily than fundamentalist terrorism or war with its neighbors. Sadder but not necessarily wiser for the experience of November 4, 1995, they are also prepared to believe the worst of themselves. As many as 70 to 80 percent of the respondents in public opinion polls believe that a political assassination can recur. (Between 18 and 24 percent of the respondents in other polls have said that they support, or at least do not oppose, a pardon for Yigal Amir.) More than 50 percent of Israel's citizens believe that the country's leaders have not drawn the necessary conclusions from the Rabin assassination. When a Gallup poll done for *Ma'ariv* on the second anniversary of the murder asked whether the country was closer to unity or civil war, more than twice as many respondents (56 compared with 21 percent) answered the latter. Four months later the Tami Steinmetz Center for Peace Research asked Israelis to rate the issues on which there is a "high chance of violence breaking out." Almost four-fifths (79 percent) of the respondents cited relations between the secular and religious camps, with friction between the left and the right coming in a close second (70 percent).

How should we interpret these disturbing data? All we can say is that as the state celebrates its jubilee year, scholars of the Jewish past and present are divided on their assessment of the future. One school views the murder of Prime Minister Rabin, the election of Prime Minister Netanyahu, and the derailing of the Oslo process as a progression that augurs the demise of Zionism as a classically secular, democratic movement. Noting that the messianic strain in Israeli life is growing increasingly militant, the members of this school see compromise with the extremists as unlikely. One of them, Hebrew University sociologist Professor Moshe Lissak, has gone so far as to characterize the secular Jewish state established in 1948 as "largely a fleeting episode."

The opposing school takes a more sanguine view. It argues that the present crisis, though particularly grave, does not necessarily foreshadow the collapse of the original Zionist design. Instead, secular Zionism will rally and begin working toward a kind of synthesis with the fundamentalist forces in Judaism. As Professor Yaron Ezrachi, a Hebrew University political scientist, writes in his 1997 book *Rubber Bullets:*

> If the agreements with our Arab neighbors indeed reduce regional tensions and the sense of siege in Israel, the focus of the relations between religion and politics may shift from issues of territories,

settlements, and power to the related yet more complex issues of values, culture, and identities. As a civilization Judaism cannot be reduced to religion (certainly not to Orthodox Judaism) and as a way of life democracy cannot be reduced to a set of political and legal procedures. The more direct encounter between Judaism and democracy in Israel is likely to trigger processes of selection and adaptation that could transform them both.

Yet this development too is predicated on the assumption that Israel must settle its conflict with its neighbors before it can resolve its dispute with itself.

The Price of Peace

Finally, the optimists believe that Israel's elites have essentially accepted the historic decision to share the Land of Israel with the Palestinians. The debate now, they say, is not over the principle of making peace but merely over the price as measured in territory.

Aryeh Naor, who as government secretary under Prime Minister [Menachem] Begin was an outspoken champion of the settlement movement and has since had a change of heart, is a prime example of this thinking. He believes that Yigal Amir's attempt to redirect the course of history with three bullets has already proved a failure. For not only does Israel's recognition of the [Palestinian Liberation Organization] remain in place, but the post-Oslo right-wing government has withdrawn from most of Hebron—the place of deepest Jewish significance in the West Bank—and has pledged to carry out further withdrawals from the occupied territories. Thus on the second anniversary of the assassination Naor was moved to write:

> The mutual recognition reached in the Oslo agreement is a recognition of reality. Peace follows from the recognition of reality, is an imperative of reality, and thus will overcome obstacles and inhibitions. The sun will yet rise to lighten the morning, and when we together bring the coveted day, we will all—Jews and Arabs, Israelis and Palestinians—stand before the grave of the late Yitzhak Rabin, the victor in war and in peace, and say: Thank you.

That day, if it ever arrives, will come too late for Yitzhak Rabin. We cannot predict how he will be remembered by his country. But in a speech to the U.S. Congress in July 1994 Rabin gave a clue about the epitaph he would have written for himself in saying: "I, military I.D. number 30743, retired general in the Israel Defense Forces in the past, consider myself to be a soldier in the army of peace today." Whether or not Yitzhak Rabin is remembered as a soldier of peace and a bold statesman who made hard decisions for the sake of his country's future will depend largely upon the kind of society Israel's citizens forge for themselves and for posterity.

The Medical and Scientific Significance of Dolly's Birth

by Marie A. DiBerardino

In early 1997 Ian Wilmut and his colleagues at the Roslin Institute in Scotland announced that on July 5, 1996, a sheep had given birth to the first mammal created from a cloned adult cell—a ewe named Dolly. The medical implications of Dolly's birth were astounding: This new knowledge could be used to treat maladies like cystic fibrosis, hemophilia, AIDS, mad cow disease, and aid in organ transplants and the eradication of birth defects by enabling scientists to reprogram mature cells and turn them into other cell types required for repair. For example, doctors will one day be able to use cloning techniques to replace a patient's damaged heart or brain cells by reprogramming the patient's own skin cells to take over.

However, the firestorm of controversy that arose over the ethics of cloning and how the technology may be misused quickly overshadowed the medical and scientific promise of Wilmut's work. Many worried that this newfound knowledge would lead to apocalyptic scenarios such as the cloning of human beings (which might be used for spare parts), the creation of designer children, the cloning of the dead, and the cloning of political despots like Adolf Hitler and Saddam Hussein. Those who support a global moratorium on cloning research believe that, despite good intentions, approval of cloning practices, even to attempt to cure genetic defects and disease, would inevitably lead to outright replication of humans. Many of these critics contend that the difference between therapeutic cloning and the cloning of full human beings is a matter of semantics. Wilmut himself believes that the cloning of humans is unethical, and he has expressed concern that this knowledge may be used by individuals with less than scrupulous intentions. Wilmut, however, does not want to see the important benefits of his research go to waste. The potential negative consequences of cloning have led some nations, including the United States, to suspend government funding for cloning research. Private funding, however, has enabled some cloning studies to continue.

In the following essay Marie A. DiBerardino, professor emerita of biochemistry at the Medical College of Pennsylvania–Hahnemann School of Medicine, explores the influence Dolly's birth will have on the future of medicine and the role that cloning plays in the future treatment of disease.

J immy walks into the neighborhood pharmacy to fill his prescription for a protein he was born without. He lacks the gene for blood clotting factor IX and relies on the local drugstore for his medicine. Jimmy pulls open the bag that contains his 90-day supply of patches, removes the old patch from his chest, and attaches a new one. He adjusts his jersey and heads out to meet his buddies for a game of touch football. Even though he is hemophiliac, Jimmy isn't worried about the bruises and scrapes he is sure to get.

Similarly,

- Christine is scheduled to have her *own* genetically reprogrammed skin cells transplanted to replace her severely damaged heart cells.
- Margo, who has Parkinson's disease, receives special nerve cells. She is not concerned about tissue incompatibility and rejection, because these cells are her own genetically reprogrammed skin cells.
- Patients routinely buy anti-cancer or anti-viral drugs in large quantities to treat their conditions.

This is the future. It is what Dolly so wondrously has wrought. Born July 1996, she is the first mammal successfully cloned from an adult cell, one taken from a ewe's mammary gland.

Nuclear Transfer

Dolly was not created in the ordinary way. Typically, a lamb is the product of natural reproduction—two germ cells, a sperm from an adult male and an egg (oocyte) from an adult female, fuse at fertilization. Each of these germ cells (the sperm and the oocyte) contributes half the chromosomes needed to create a new individual. Chromosomes are found in the cell's nucleus and they carry the DNA, which is the genetic blueprint for an individual.

The process that produced Dolly differs from ordinary reproduction in two major ways. First, body (or somatic) cells from an adult ewe's udder (this is the donor) were placed in a culture dish and allowed to grow. The nutrients were then removed from the culture, which stopped the cells' growth. One of these non-growing cells was then fused (by electric jolts) with another ewe's oocyte from which the nucleus had been previously removed (i.e., enucleated, so it had no chromosomes). This procedure is known as 'somatic cell nuclear transfer'. Within a day the fused cells began to divide in the culture dish. After several divisions, the early embryo was transferred to the uterus of a surrogate mother and allowed to develop.

Second, unlike the sperm and the egg, each of which contributes half the number of chromosomes at fertilization, each body cell contains twice the number of chromosomes in each germ cell. So fusion of a sperm and an egg forms an individual whose full genetic composition is unique to that individual. On the other hand, the embryo cloned from somatic cell nuclear transfer begins development with the diploid (double) number of chromosomes, all derived from one somatic cell (adult udder) of a single individual. This embryo has the same nuclear genetic composition as the donor of the somatic cell.

In the end, three sheep contributed to the production of a single lamb clone: a Finn Dorset sheep donated her udder cells for culture; a Scottish Blackface sheep donated the enucleated oocyte (with its nucleus removed, thus losing its own genetic identity in the process); and a Scottish Blackface sheep became the surrogate mother, carrying the embryo to birth. The clone (Dolly) was easily identified because she had the physical traits of the Finn Dorset sheep that donated the udder cells and differed from the traits of the Scottish Blackface sheep used as the surrogate mother and the oocyte donor.

And now Dolly herself is a mother—the old-fashioned way—

by mating with David, a Welsh mountain ram, and giving birth to Bonnie. In fact, Bonnie now has other siblings.

Imagine herds of female sheep, cattle, and goats producing large quantities of human proteins in their milk, an ideal place for those proteins to be harvested and used to treat patients like Jimmy, the hemophiliac, whose blood cannot clot. We can realize this dream today—one step at a time, because the process that produced Dolly also can be used to produce the transgenic (one species carrying another species' genes) clones.

Scottish scientists first removed cells from a fetal lamb and grew them in a culture dish. Multiple copies of fragments of DNA (deoxyribonucleic acid, which holds genetic information) containing the human gene for blood clotting factor IX were added to the dish and coaxed into the cells. Some cells incorporated the human DNA into their chromosomes, thus becoming 'transgenic cells', or cells containing a transferred gene.

These transgenic cells were then separated from those without human DNA and used to create Polly, the transgenic sheep that today produces the human clotting factor IX in her milk. Purposely, scientists genetically designed the transgenic sheep clones so that the human gene would function only in the mammary gland.

It will soon be possible for the human clotting factor IX protein to be routinely harvested and purified from the sheep milk. Obviously, researchers still need to conduct controlled clinical studies before this protein is available for hemophiliacs like Jimmy, but they have already made an astonishing breakthrough.

Transgenic Clones

The importance of the transgenic clones is that biotechnology is now being extended to produce different human proteins like insulin (diabetes), interferon (viral infections), clotting factor VIII (hemophilia), and tissue plasminogen activator (dissolving blood clots). In other words, female clones of such animals as cattle, sheep, and goats are being genetically designed to be dairy/pharmaceutical producers, a virtual living bio-pharmaceutical industry. Transgenic clones of mammals are a major advance in biotechnology because they can synthesize, in large quantities, complex molecules critically required for patient care. The current recombinant DNA technology in bacteria is capable of synthesizing only simple proteins, but not the complex molecules that sheep can produce in large quantities in their milk. Indeed, Jimmy will be able to wear his patch very soon.

While these advances are on the horizon for us, beneficial applications to agriculture are already being implemented. Transgenic cloning can be used for the genetic improvement of livestock related to milk production, quality of meat, growth rate, reproduction, nutrition, behavioral traits, and/or resistance to diseases. This cloning process simply accelerates the older, slower, and less predictable methods of crossbreeding and hybridization.

Strictly speaking, clones obtained from nuclear transfer are not exact copies of the donor. A clone like Dolly produced by oocyte-somatic cell fusion is a mosaic—a mixture of the oocyte and body cell. In addition to the nucleus, the donor cell contributes a tiny amount of cytoplasm and cell membrane to the oocyte, but the egg cell contributes an enormous amount of cytoplasm and cell membrane to the fused product. In fact, virtually all mitochondria (the organelles in the cytoplasm that are the major source of cell energy and contain DNA of their own) are derived from the oocyte cytoplasm. So cloning of multicellular organisms is not equal to true cellular cloning that results from asexual reproduction, when a one-celled organism like the amoeba divides and clones itself.

Similarly, plants clone themselves when they reproduce by budding or sprouting new shoots. The agricultural industry has intentionally propagated—by cloning—bananas, grapes, apples, sugar cane, pineapples, potatoes, asparagus, and many other plants. Identical twins and triplets that occur among many multicellular animal species including humans, are derived by a cloning process. A cell, isolated from other cells growing in a culture dish, gives rise after cell division to a clone. All these examples include the exact duplication of the whole body cell, including the nucleus, cytoplasm, and cell membrane.

Why Is This Such a Big Deal?

Dolly has debunked a long-held, generally accepted biological concept: Adult cells have their fate sealed; put another way, once an udder cell, always an udder cell. This means that the genetic status of the adult donor nucleus had to be reprogrammed, and that the oocyte cytoplasm seems to contain the appropriate molecules to trigger this reprogramming. The value of cloning from an adult cell is that we can predict that the clone will be very much like the donor animal, whereas we cannot do so when the clone is derived from an embryonic or fetal cell. Even when the parents of embryos and fetuses are known, we cannot yet foretell exactly the physical traits of their offspring; they are a combination of traits from both parents. Additional variations occur because, during the maturation of the parents' sperm and egg before fertilization, the genes are randomly distributed to sperm and egg cells. Thus, offspring cloned from adult cells are more similar to their donor than are offspring that result from sexual reproduction, i.e., a combination of sperm and egg. There is, however, no guarantee that an exact copy will evolve, because variations in the physical traits of the donor may result from environmental influences during pre- and postnatal development and, in some cases, from the mitochondrial DNA of the oocyte.

Totipotency

Animal cloning began more than a century ago when scientists wondered how an initially formless mass of cells, the blastocyst, develops into a structured organism composed of separate skin cells, blood cells, muscle cells, brain cells, stomach cells, and so on. They specifically wanted to know whether these many different cell types were irreversible or whether these differentiated cells could reverse and express again the totipotency of the early embryo.

Early Embryonic Cells Are Totipotent—By using an early version of the nuclear transfer technique in their initial studies, scientists established that nuclei from early embryonic cells were indeed totipotent; that is, they could develop into complete fertile organisms, with all the cell types and organs of an adult. These studies showed that frogs, salamanders, insects, fish, and mammals (mice, rats, rabbits, pigs, goats, cattle, and sheep) could be produced by this process. Furthermore, many of these species were fertile. (The only primates to have been cloned by nuclear transfer thus far are two Rhesus monkeys produced from the nuclei of an eight-cell stage embryo.)

Few Nuclei Remain Totipotent Throughout Development—Scientists now know that the older the donor cell from which the nucleus is transplanted, the more likely it is that the injected oocyte will develop abnormally. In fact, only a few tadpole nuclei from frogs have been shown to be totipotent, and those may have come from immature cells. When fully differentiated cell types (pigment, skin, red and white blood cells) from adult frogs were used as donors, their nuclei gave rise to tadpoles but not to fertile frogs. In mammals, very few *fetal* cell nuclei (approximately 0.3–2%) from sheep and cattle led to the normal development of living newborn animals. Dolly, produced from an *adult* cell, represents only a 0.2% cloning success. The inability to clone most nuclei from advanced stages probably results from protein changes that occur in the chromosomes during cell differentiation, changes that will have to be identified and controlled in the future.

Genetic Reprogramming

Scientists found that cloning actually reprograms nuclear function and returns some nuclei to an undifferentiated state. This discovery followed a line of basic research that may result in some of the most beneficial applications to humans.

Soon after a nucleus is transferred to an egg, there occurs a two-way transfer of specific proteins between the nucleus and cytoplasm. This transfer causes modifications in chromosomal proteins, resulting in nuclear DNA synthesis, and later in the expression of a new set of genes. These and other changes reflect reprogramming of nuclear function by chemicals in the oocyte cytoplasm. When investigators identify the role of these proteins, we will understand how to convert a nucleus from a differentiated adult cell type into one that is relatively immature. This might permit us to actually *reprogram* mature cells and turn them into specific cell types required for tissue repair. By doing this, we could potentially replace damaged heart or brain cells by reprogramming the patients' own skin cells into heart muscle cells and nerve cells (for people like Christine and Margo).

Dolly Is Only the First!

Dolly is no longer unique, although she always will be the first animal cloned from an adult cell. Being the result of a nuclear transfer between an adult ewe udder cell and an enucleated oocyte, she showed that an adult mammalian cell could be reprogrammed genetically to be totipotent and give rise to an entire individual that grew to maturity and gave birth to offspring of her own. Soon after Dolly was born, a set of triplet transgenic calves bearing a foreign gene was cloned from fetal cells, all sharing the same nuclear genes. This indicates the feasibility of producing herds of sheep and cattle capable of producing the same protein.

In Hawaii, 17 months after the announcement of Dolly's birth, 32 mice were cloned from cumulus cells (i.e., cells that surround the developing oocytes in the ovaries), confirming successful cloning from adult cells. Ten of these clones have themselves produced normal progeny, and some of the 31 clones themselves came from clones, demonstrating the feasibility of augmenting the number of clones. In December 1998, eight calves were cloned from a single adult cow's cumulus and oviductal cells (cells lining the tubes of the oviduct that transport oocytes to the uterus). These studies showed that not only adult cells could be reprogrammed, but also that some differentiated cells (such as cumulus and oviductal cells) had the same capability. Keep in mind that not all adult cells are differentiated; for example, undifferentiated cells are found in bone marrow, the intestinal lining, etc., of adults.

Direct Advantages

Transgenic clones can be directly beneficial to humans, other animals, and agriculture in additional ways.

- They may be developed for tissue and organ transplantation. Although not yet a reality, there is promise that large animals can be genetically designed and cloned so that their tissues and organs will not trigger immunological responses in the recipient and cause them to be rejected. Recently, muscle rigidity and tremors in parkinsonian rats were improved by transplanting cloned transgenic bovine neurons into their brains. This research, called xenotransplantation, is one of the many avenues being pursued in an attempt to alleviate the desperate shortage of human tissues for transplantation.
- Domestic animals can be genetically designed to express a certain human disease and therefore serve as models for the study and treatment of human illnesses. Although many mouse models of human diseases are available today, such models in large domestic animals physiologically more similar to humans are sparse and critically needed.
- Somatic cell nuclear transfer might help preserve endangered species such as pandas that have low reproductive rates.

Indirect Advantages

Two other significant gains from clones are worth mentioning.

First, inducing cancer cells to differentiate is a useful type of therapy. We know that many types of cancer cells are less specialized than their normal counterparts. For this reason investigators suspected that the precursors of cancer cells could be immature cells or stem cells that fail to complete differentiation. If this is so, then by using information gained from nuclear transfer technology, we may be able to induce the cells to mature and stop making tumors. Previous studies have demonstrated that we can control at least some cancer cells by using the differentiation process.

Second, aged cell nuclei can be rejuvenated. People and other organisms change as they age. Environmental insults and diseases cause these changes; others are intrinsic to the organism. Studies using cell culture have shown that body cells grow and divide normally in culture for awhile, but eventually stop dividing, become senescent, and die. An exception was seen in aged frog red blood cell nuclei (human red blood cells lack nuclei): After their transfer into enucleated oocytes, frog red blood cell nuclei were rejuvenated. They carried out the formation of tadpoles that survived almost a third of the way to metamorphosis. The oocyte cytoplasm contains an abundance of chemicals that promote DNA synthesis and cell division after normal fertilization. We believe that these substances also rejuvenate aged cell nuclei and turn non-cycling frog red blood cells into active ones. If we could isolate these substances, we might be able to alleviate—or reverse—senescence.

Perils

Although Dolly, mice, and calves have been the first animals cloned from adult cells, the low efficiency in producing them negates attempts to clone humans. The Dolly experiment began with 434 attempts to fuse a mammary gland cell to an oocyte, and ended with only a 0.2% success rate; the remaining attempts resulted in death either during fusion or in various developmental stages. Moreover, the 1–2% success rate with mouse and 1–5% with calf cloning from adult cells are equally low. And high frequency of fetal (approximately 60%) and neonatal (approximately 50%) deaths are common. In a real sense, cloning is a roulette game.

Even if cloning from adult cells did become efficient, there still would be serious hazards.

- Donor cells could suffer mutations from radiation, chemicals, aging, and/or errors in DNA replication during the lifetime of the donor, which would be transferred to the clone.
- Mutations could arise in donor cells during cell culture, not an unusual event, and there is no way of distinguishing a normal donor cell from a mutant one.
- The embryo may be a mosaic of cells, some with apparently normal chromosomes and others with abnormal ones. So far, the prospects for identifying an abnormal embryo prior to transfer to the uterus are poor.

And there are other scientific concerns:

- the life span of the clone is unknown, as is
- the compatibility between the genetic products in the cytoplasm of the oocyte and the donor cell, and
- during the normal process of sexual reproduction, there is a natural selection of the fittest germ cells in fertilization. Although this process is not perfect (i.e., it fails to eliminate some harmful mutations), it does not exist in cloning.

So we can see that it is unlikely that cloning of a human being from any donor age will happen any time soon. Indeed, the scientific community was so strongly opposed to the production of a human being by cloning techniques that the Federation of American Societies for Experimental Biology and other professional organizations representing more than 67,000 scientists have issued a voluntary moratorium against such an act. The groups endorsing this position included those scientists most capable of performing this type of work.

Although these scientists believe that cloning a human being is unethical and reprehensible, they are still concerned that some of the anti-cloning legislation designed to prevent the cloning of a human being contains language that also will prohibit vital biomedical research that can lead to the repair of diseased and damaged human tissues and organs, and to possible treatments and cures for diabetes, cancer, Parkinson's disease, and other neurodegenerative diseases.

Other nations have found a successful balance between these two concerns. Many European countries have outlawed attempts to clone humans, while preserving the freedom of scientists pursuing cloning studies in non-human organisms because of the potential benefits. In the United States, the National Bioethics Advisory Committee recommended an "imposed period of time in which no attempt is made to create a child using somatic cell nuclear transfer." In their 1997 statement, the committee cautioned, "Any regulatory or legislative actions undertaken to effect the foregoing prohibition on creating a child by somatic cell nuclear transfer should be carefully written so as not to interfere with other important areas of scientific research."

Knowledge: Threat or Promise?

When scientists first discovered anesthesia, atomic energy, and recombinant DNA, we did not know if these breakthroughs might lead to deleterious applications. The choices we make for the application of knowledge reside in ethical decisions by humans. Animal cloning, like other research, was initiated to seek fundamental knowledge for the benefit of humankind. In addition to expanding the knowledge base in cellular, developmental, and molecular biology, as well as in cancer and aging, cloning has now been applied to enhance medicine and agriculture. Presently, hospital committees in the United States bar attempts to clone humans because of clinical, safety, and ethical concerns. Cloning is only one of many discoveries in which society will have to choose which applications are ethical and which ones are not.

Ian Wilmut Addresses the Questions Raised by Dolly's Birth

by Andrew Ross

The following interview was conducted by journalist Andrew Ross in the immediate wake of the announcement of Dolly's birth. Ross interviews Ian Wilmut, an embryologist at the Roslin Institute in Edinburgh, Scotland, as he attempts to allay fears that his recent discovery will lead to the outright cloning of human beings. Wilmut points out that his achievement will change the way that doctors treat disease and birth defects and that the benefits borne of this discovery will far outweigh any potential risks. Although Wilmut argues that the outright cloning of human beings is so far from being a reality that it does not warrant the hysteria that it generates, he does express concern that the knowledge could fall into the wrong hands and be used for less-than-honorable reasons.

"**R**esearchers Astounded. . . . Fiction Becomes True and Dreaded Possibilities Are Raised." So went the headlines in [the] *New York Times* about Dr. Ian Wilmut, the embryologist in Edinburgh who has made history by creating a lamb from the DNA of an adult sheep. The research, performed at the Roslin Institute in Edinburgh, was sponsored by

---

a drug company, PPL Therapeutics.

Dr. Wilmut says the primary purpose of the cloning is to advance the development of drug therapies to combat certain life-threatening human diseases. Other scientists, especially in the United States, appear to have adopted a more apocalyptic view of the news. "It basically means there are no limits," Dr. Lee Silver, a biologist at Princeton University, told the *New York Times*. "It means all of science fiction is true." Dr. Ronald Munson, a medical ethicist at the University of Missouri, said, "This technology is not, in principle, policeable." Munson even speculated about the possibility of cloning the dead.

Are such scenarios remotely possible? And if drug treatment is the main priority, how soon will we see animal clone–based drugs on the market? Salon spoke with Wilmut by telephone from his home in Edinburgh.

Andrew Ross: *Science fiction. Cloning the dead. A technology out of control. What do you make of such reactions to your work?*

Ian Wilmut: I think they're over the top. The point is that what we thought happens in all life is that you have a single fertilized egg and as it divides, it progressively differentiates and you get brain and muscle and all of the different kinds of cells that we have. People assumed until now that this was an irreversible process. And what we have shown is that it's not. Now people will have to think in slightly different ways about the mechanisms that control these changes—for example, about what happens when things go wrong and you get a cancer instead of a normal development. So it is going to open people's eyes a lot in terms of biology.

And does it mean that cloning humans is possible?

We don't know. It is quite likely that it is possible, yes. But what we've said all along—speaking for both the (Roslin) Institute and the PPL staff—is that we would find it ethically unacceptable to think of doing that. We can't think of a reason to do it. If there was a reason to copy a human being, we would do it, but there isn't.

Is the idea of cloning the dead totally fanciful?

Yep.

Still, even if you can't clone the dead and you see no reason to clone the living, the genie is out of the bottle, so to speak. Others might find reasons for human cloning, and they may not have the same standard of ethics as you.

That does worry me, both in principle and in detail. It worries me in detail because the successes we have at present are of such low efficiency that it would really be quite appalling to think of doing that with people. I would feel desperately sorry for the women and the children that were involved.

Why? Because the clone could turn out to be some kind of monster?

It's possible. Perhaps you don't know that in the first experiment that we reported, five lambs were born alive and three of them died quickly. There was nothing monstrous, they just simply died. That in itself is very distressing if you think of a mother who carries a child and it dies within a few days of birth.

The Benefits of Cloning

Your main goal, you have said, is to develop health-related products from animal clones. In what areas, specifically?

Hemophilia. With animals, you could make the clotting factors which are missing. It could also be beneficial for cystic fibrosis.

What's the difference between using animal clones and other kinds of biotechnology techniques?

Speed and efficiency. You could take cells from an animal, grow them in the laboratory and make very precise genetic changes—it's called gene targeting—which you insert in the cloned offspring. So, for example, you put into the cells of the offspring DNA sequences which would say, "Don't make this particular milk protein, but instead make clotting factor 8," which is needed for hemophilia. You can do that now, but by using a much more primitive technique. Cloning and gene targeting requires fewer animals. It will be quicker, which means new health products will come on line more quickly.

There's another major advantage. Presuming this technique with sheep will successfully extend to cattle and then to pigs, it will speed xeno-transplantation—using organs from pigs to treat human patients. That can be done now, but what happens now is that you put a human protein into the pig organ which kind of damps down the immune response in the transplant patient. Now with gene targeting, we can do that, but we can also change the *surface* of the cells, so that they would be less antigenic when the pig organ is put into a human patient—which makes it more likely that organ transplantation will work.

So, instead of waiting for a human donor, we'll be seeing many more animal organ-to-human transplants.
Yes, with pig organs in particular.
And who would be helped the most?
Well, there is a need for more hearts and more kidneys. At present people die before human hearts can be made available to them.
There have been attempts to use baboon transplants in AIDS patients.
Yes, but people feel it's more acceptable to think of using pigs because baboons seem so much more—
—human?
That's right. Aware of their environment.

Repairing Genetic Defects

With animal cloning research, will it be possible to go in and fix genetic defects in humans? For example, there are already tests for a predisposition to breast cancer.
I think that is so far away that it's not really credible. I mean you're quite right theoretically. But the efficiencies we have at the present time and our understanding are so naive and primitive that you wouldn't contemplate doing it. I think we could contribute in a smaller way to certain genetic diseases—breast cancer is not one that I've thought of—but, for example, with cystic fibrosis. It has been suggested that we study the role of the gene which is defective in people who suffer from cystic fibrosis with the hope that better therapies can be developed. We could also provide model test animals in which methods of gene therapy can be developed.
Which is being done with mice.
Yes, but mice are so different and so small that experimentation is very difficult. Sheep would be much more appropriate.
Do you see a therapy for cystic fibrosis based on animal clones in your lifetime?
Yes. I'm 52, I reckon I've got 20 years. I'm fairly comfortable predicting we'll see something in that time period.
In addition to drug therapy for humans, your research has major implications for animals.
Yes, it may open a whole range of things we can't imagine at the present time. Remember, we only know about what, 5 or 10 percent of the animal genes? But there is a particular project

which is of immediate relevance in Britain concerning the disease scrapie.

Mad Cow Disease?

That's right. What people believe is that the agent which causes scrapie in sheep causes BSE (Bovine Spongiform Encephalitis) in cows and some of the CJD (Creuzfeld-Jacob Disease) in humans. It is believed to start with a particular gene in sheep. Now what if we could modify that gene; could we make sheep that are resistant to scrapie? That's very important for sheep, but also for BSE and CJD in humans.

When?

Twenty years or so.

There is also talk of "supercows" producing enormous quantities of milk. Could it be made cholesterol-free, by the way?

There are all sorts of questions like that. The answer to them is, we don't know. One thing I would say is that history shows that people are very bad at predicting the way that technology will be used.

Any implications for world hunger?

Not immediately. But if we can maybe make animals resistant to some diseases—to the tsetse fly, for example—it is quite possible that we can contribute to a whole range of things.

Ethical Concerns

You've been working on this project for 10 years. Did you ever ask yourself, "Am I Dr. Frankenstein here? I know what I want to achieve but am I contributing to something I don't want to see happen?"

Of course. And we've tried to have this information released responsibly to journalists like yourself, to ethicists, to people concerned with legislation, because what we want is to stimulate an informed public discussion of the way in which the techniques might be misused as well as used and to ensure legislation was put in place to prevent misuse. But what we're also concerned with as well is that we don't throw the baby out with the bathwater. There are real potential benefits, and it's important that the concern to prevent misuse doesn't also prevent the really useful benefits that can be gained from this research.

What misuse are you most concerned with?

Any kind of manipulation with human embryos should be prohibited.

Are you concerned that your work will be stopped?

I have some concerns about it. I totally understand that people find this sort of research offensive, and I respect their views. It's also possible for a minority to have very large influence. Now, if society says it doesn't want us to do this kind of research, well, that's fine. But I think it has to be an overall view made by an informed population.

Assuming it goes forward, when will we see the first concrete applications?

I think there will be animals on the ground with interesting new products in three years. I think we'll come up with clotting factors, possibly in cattle as well as in sheep. Of course there will be a long time for testing the products before they go into commercial use. But there will be animals that are able to secrete new proteins, different proteins, in three years.

CHRONOLOGY

1980

January 4: In protest over the Soviet invasion of Afghanistan, U.S. president Jimmy Carter announces American boycott of the Summer Olympics in Moscow.

April 24: Eight American servicemen die in a failed attempt to rescue hostages held by Islamic radicals in Tehran, Iran.

May 18: Mount Saint Helens erupts in Washington. The blast levels over 150 square miles of forest and sends a plume of smoke and ash 15 miles into the sky.

September 22: Iraq invades Iran.

November 4: Ronald Reagan is elected U.S. president.

1981

January 20: American hostages being held in Iran are released minutes after Ronald Reagan is sworn in as president.

March 30: John W. Hinckley Jr. attempts to assassinate President Ronald Reagan. The president is shot but quickly recovers.

June 5: AIDS is first identified by Dr. Michael Gottlieb in an article that appears in *Morbidity and Mortality Weekly Report*.

August 1: MTV begins broadcasting.

August 12: The IBM personal computer (PC) debuts.

September 25: Sandra Day O'Connor, the first woman appointed to the U.S. Supreme Court, is sworn in.

October 6: Egyptian president Anwar Sadat is assassinated by Muslim extremists in Cairo.

December 13: Solidarity leaders are arrested in Poland, and marshal law is declared.

December 14: Israel annexes the Golan Heights, an area taken from Syria during the Six-Day War in 1967.

1982

April 2: Argentina invades the Falkland Islands, touching off a brief and disastrous war with Great Britain.

June 6: Israel invades Lebanon.

October 1: The compact disc is unveiled by CBS/Sony in Japan.
November 10: Soviet leader Leonid Brezhnev dies. He is succeeded by Yuri Andropov.
November 16: The space shuttle *Columbia* makes its first mission.
December 2: The first permanent artificial heart is implanted in Barney Clark at the University of Utah Medical Center in Salt Lake City.

1983
January 23: Dr. Luc Montagnier isolates the virus that causes AIDS.
March 23: In a nationally televised address, President Ronald Reagan announces plans to build the Strategic Defense Initiative (Star Wars) weapons system.
June 18: Sally K. Ride becomes the first American woman to go into space.
August 30: A South Korean passenger jet strays into Soviet airspace and is shot down; all 269 passengers are killed.
October 23: A terrorist truck bomb explodes at U.S. Marine headquarters in Beirut, Lebanon, killing 225 Americans.

1984
February 7: President Reagan withdraws U.S. troops from the international peacekeeping force in Lebanon.
May 7: The Soviet Union announces that it will not attend the Summer Olympics in Los Angeles.
September 4: Indian prime minister Indira Gandhi is assassinated by two of her bodyguards.
November 7: Toxic gas leaks from a Union Carbide plant in Bhopal, India, killing 2,000 and injuring 150,000.

1985
March 11: Mikhail Gorbachev becomes leader of the Soviet Union and initiates a broad range of reforms under the banners of glasnost and perestroika.
July 13: The Live Aid concert, held simultaneously in London and Philadelphia, raises almost $70 million for starving people in Africa.
October 2: Actor Rock Hudson dies of AIDS. He is the first high-profile casualty of the epidemic.

1986

January 28: The space shuttle *Challenger* explodes after take-off, killing all seven crew members.
April 26: An explosion occurs at the nuclear power plant in the Ukraine city of Chernobyl, igniting the worst nuclear reactor disaster in history. Eight tons of radioactive material escaped into the atmosphere, and some estimates indicate that as many as eight thousand people died.

1987

March 19: Azidothymidine (AZT) wins FDA approval for the treatment of AIDS.
May 5: Iran-Contra hearings begin.
October 19: The stock market crashes on what becomes known as Black Monday. In the worst single-day decline in its history, the Dow Jones plunges 508 points.
December 8: Widespread rioting erupts among Palestinians living in the Israeli-occupied territories. The six-year uprising becomes known as the *Intifada.* At a summit in Washington, D.C., President Reagan and Mikhail Gorbachev sign the Intermediate-Range Nuclear Forces (INF) Treaty, the first in which the two superpowers commit to dismantling an entire class of nuclear missiles.

1988

February 4: The U.S. grand jury indicts Panamanian leader Manuel Noriega on drug charges.
November 8: George Bush defeats Michael Dukakis in the U.S. presidential election.
December 1: Benazir Bhutto becomes prime minister of Pakistan. She is the first woman chosen to lead an Islamic nation.
December 21: A terrorist bomb destroys Pan Am Flight 487 as it passes over Lockerbie, Scotland. All 259 passengers, as well as 11 people on the ground, are killed.

1989

March 24: The *Exxon Valdez* runs aground in Alaska, spilling millions of barrels of oil into Prince William Sound.
June 4: Chinese troops crush prodemocracy student demonstration in Tiananmen Square in Beijing.

June 5: In the first free elections in forty years, voters in Poland bring an end to Communist rule.

November 9: East Germany opens its border with West Germany, and jubilant crowds begin to tear down the Berlin Wall.

November 30: The Czech Parliament ends the dominant role of the Communist Party.

December 15: An uprising in Romania deposes the Communist regime of Nicolae Ceausescu. Ceausescu and his wife are executed ten days later.

December 20: U.S. troops invade Panama seeking to capture Manuel Noriega.

1990

January 22: Communists are deposed in Yugoslavia.

February 4: Mass rallies and strikes are held in Moscow to protest Communist rule in the Soviet Union.

February 11: After more than twenty-seven years of incarceration, antiapartheid activist Nelson Mandela is freed from prison in South Africa.

April 25: The Hubble Space Telescope is launched.

August 2: Iraqi troops invade Kuwait.

August 16: In a mission called Operation Desert Shield, tens of thousands of U.S. troops arrive in Saudi Arabia to prepare to drive Iraqi forces from Kuwait.

August 31: East and West Germany reunite.

1991

January 16: An international coalition of allied air forces led by the United States begins a massive bombing campaign on Iraqi positions to begin Operation Desert Storm.

February 28: The Gulf War officially ends; Kuwait's independence is restored, but Saddam Hussein remains in power in Iraq.

June 4: The Communist regime in Albania resigns.

June 5: The South African Parliament repeals apartheid laws.

June 6: Boris Yeltsin is elected president of the Russian republic.

June 25: Civil war erupts in Yugoslavia as the republics of Slovenia and Croatia declare independence.

July 1: The Warsaw Pact is dissolved.

August 19–21: Mikhail Gorbachev is briefly overthrown by Communist hard-liners.

August 29: The Soviet legislature suspends all activities of the

Communist Party; this is the first time in seventy years that the Soviet Union is not ruled by Communists.

December 12: Tim Berners-Lee and Robert Cailliau deploy the first World Wide Web server.

December 25: Gorbachev resigns and transfers power to Russian president Yeltsin; the Soviet Union is dissolved and replaced with a commonwealth of independent states.

1992

February 29: Fighting spreads in the Yugoslavian civil war as Bosnia-Herzegovina declares its independence.

April 29: The acquittal of four police officers accused of beating Rodney King ignites widespread rioting in Los Angeles.

November 2: Bill Clinton wins the U.S. presidency.

December 9: U.S. troops land in Somalia to deliver humanitarian aid.

1993

February 11: Janet Reno becomes the first woman appointed attorney general of the United States.

February 26: The World Trade Center is bombed by four men associated with radical Islamic terrorist groups.

February 28: The Bureau of Alcohol, Tobacco, and Firearms attempts to serve a warrant on the Branch Davidian religious sect in Waco, Texas. In the resulting shootout, six federal officers are killed and sixteen are wounded while six Branch Davidians are killed.

April 19: The standoff between federal agents and the Branch Davidians ends with a firestorm that kills eighty people.

September 13: Israeli prime minister Yitzhak Rabin and Palestine Liberation Organization (PLO) chairman Yasser Arafat sign the Oslo accords. The agreement provides for Israeli withdrawal from the Gaza Strip and Jericho and recognition of the PLO.

November 18: South Africa adopts a majority-rule constitution.

1994

February 28: The North Atlantic Treaty Organization (NATO) begins its first offensive in Bosnia when U.S. jet fighters, enforcing a "no-fly" zone over central Bosnia, shoot down four Serbian jets.

April 6: Ethnic Hutus begin a hundred-day campaign of terror against the Tutsi tribe in Rwanda. An estimated eight hundred thousand Tutsis are killed in the rampage.

April 29: The first multiracial elections are held in South Africa; Nelson Mandela is elected president.

August 31: The Irish Republican Army (IRA) declares ceasefire in Northern Ireland.

1995

March 14: The Russian space station *Mir* greets its first Americans.

April 19: Timothy McVeigh ignites a truck bomb in front of the Alfred P. Murrah Federal Building in Oklahoma City, killing 168 people.

November 4: Israeli prime minister Yitzhak Rabin is assassinated at a Tel Aviv peace rally.

December 14: The presidents of Bosnia, Croatia, and Serbia sign a peace accord in Paris.

1996

July 5: Dolly, a lamb cloned from the single cell of an adult sheep, is born in Scotland.

September 27: The Taliban, an organization of radical Islamic students, captures the Afghan capital of Kabul.

December 5: Madeleine Albright becomes the first woman appointed U.S. secretary of state.

1997

June 30: Hong Kong returns to Chinese rule.

August 31: Princess Diana of Wales is killed in a car accident in a Paris tunnel.

1998

March 5: Serbians attack ethnic Albanians in Kosovo.

April 10: The Good Friday Accord is signed in Northern Ireland. The accord calls for Protestants to share power with minority Catholics and gives the Republic of Ireland a voice in Northern Irish affairs.

May 3: Europeans agree on a single currency, the euro.

May 11: India conducts three atomic tests.

May 29: In response to the Indian tests, Pakistan conducts five nuclear tests.

August 7: U.S. embassies in Kenya and Tanzania are bombed by Islamic terrorists.

December 19: The House Judiciary Committee approves two articles of impeachment against President Bill Clinton, charging him with lying to a grand jury and obstructing justice by covering up his affair with White House intern Monica Lewinsky.

1999

January 7: The U.S. Senate opens the impeachment trial of President Bill Clinton.

February 12: The U.S. Senate votes 55 to 45 against convicting President Clinton of the perjury charge against him, and 50 to 50 on the obstruction of justice charge; the vote puts an end to the possibility of Clinton's removal from office.

March 24: Serbian leader Slobodan Milosevic intensifies the campaign against ethnic Albanians in the Kosovo region.

April 20: Students Eric Harris and Dylan Klebold enter Columbine High School in Littleton, Colorado, with an arsenal of high-powered firearms and bombs, killing thirteen and wounding twenty-three others before turning their guns on themselves.

October 12: The Pakistani government is overthrown by General Pervez Musharraf amid economic strife and increased hostility with India over the disputed Kashmir region.

2000

June 26: Scientists announce they have mapped the human genome.

July 2: Vicente Fox Quesada is elected president of Mexico, ending seventy-one years of one-party rule by the Institutional Revolutionary Party.

October 5: Mass public demonstrations in Yugoslavia force President Milosevic to step down.

October 12: A terrorist bomb kills seventeen U.S. sailors aboard the destroyer *Cole* during a refueling stop in Aden, Yemen.

FOR FURTHER RESEARCH

Janet Abbate, *Inventing the Internet.* Cambridge, MA: MIT Press, 1999.

Carol Barner-Barry, *The Politics of Change: The Transformation of the Former Soviet Union.* New York: St. Martin's, 1995.

Jasper Becker, *The Chinese.* New York: Free, 2000.

Phyllis Bennis, *From Stones to Statehood: The Palestinian Uprising.* Brooklyn, NY: Olive Branch, 1990.

Tim Berners-Lee, *Weaving the Web: The Original Design and Ultimate Destiny of the World Wide Web.* San Francisco: HarperSanFrancisco, 1999.

John Bulloch and Harvey Morris, *The Origins of the Kuwait Conflict and the International Response.* London: Faber & Faber, 1991.

Ian Buruma, *Bad Elements: Chinese Rebels from Los Angeles to Beijing.* New York: Random House, 2001.

Paul E. Ceruzzi, *A History of Modern Computing.* Cambridge, MA: MIT Press, 1998.

Frank Ching, *Hong Kong and China: "One Country, Two Systems"?* New York: Foreign Policy Association, 1996.

Fred Coleman, *The Decline and Fall of the Soviet Empire: Forty Years That Shook the World, from Stalin to Yeltsin.* New York: St. Martin's, 1997.

Floyd Cooper, *Mandela: From the Life of the South African Statesman.* New York: Philomel Books, 1996.

John B. Dunlop, *The Rise of Russia and the Fall of the Soviet Empire.* Princeton, NJ: Princeton University Press, 1993.

Stephen Ellmann, *In a Time of Trouble: Law and Liberty in South Africa's State of Emergency.* New York: Oxford University Press, 1992.

Andrew Goodwin, *Dancing in the Distraction Factory: Music Television and Popular Culture.* Minneapolis: University of Minnesota Press, 1992.

Richard C. Holbrooke, *To End a War.* New York: Random House, 1999.

David Hudson, *Rewired.* Indianapolis: Macmillan, 1997.

David Clay Large, *Berlin.* New York: Basic Books, 2000.

Malcolm McConnell, *"Challenger": A Major Malfunction.* Garden City, NY: Doubleday, 1987.

Zhores A. Medvedev, *The Legacy of Chernobyl.* New York: W.W. Norton, 1990.

James A.R. Miles, *The Legacy of Tiananmen: China in Disarray.* Ann Arbor: University of Michigan Press, 1996.

Luc Montagnier, *Virus: The Co-Discoverer of HIV Tracks Its Rampage and Charts the Future.* New York: W.W. Norton, 2000.

John Francis Murphy, *Sword of Islam: Muslim Extremism from the Arab Conquests to the Attack on America.* Amherst, NY: Prometheus Books, 2002.

Cindy Patton and Janis Kelly, *Making It: A Woman's Guide to Sex in the Age of AIDS.* Ithaca, NY: Firebrand Books, 1987.

Shimon Peres and Robert Littell, *For the Future of Israel.* Baltimore: Johns Hopkins University Press, 1998.

Carolyn Collins Petersen and John C. Brandt, *Hubble Vision: Further Adventures with the Hubble Space Telescope.* New York: Cambridge University Press, 1998.

Barry D. Schoub, *AIDS and HIV in Perspective: A Guide to Understanding the Virus and Its Consequences.* New York: Cambridge University Press, 1999.

Randy Shilts, *And the Band Played On: Politics, People, and the AIDS Epidemic.* New York: St. Martin's, 1987.

Laura Silber and Allan Little, *Yugoslavia: Death of a Nation.* New York: TV Books, 1995.

Lee M. Silver, *Remaking Eden: Cloning and Beyond in a Brave New World.* New York: Avon Books, 1997.

Gerald James Stine, *Acquired Immune Deficiency Syndrome: Biological, Medical, Social, and Legal Issues.* Englewood Cliffs, NJ: Prentice-Hall, 1996.

Ed Vulliamy, *Seasons in Hell: Understanding Bosnia's War.* New York: St. Martin's, 1994.

Patty Waldmeir, *Anatomy of a Miracle: The End of Apartheid and the Birth of the New South Africa.* New York: W.W. Norton, 1997.

Marc Weingarten, *Station to Station: The History of Rock 'n' Roll on Television.* New York: Pocket Books, 2000.

Ian Wilmut, *The Second Creation: Dolly and the Age of Biological Control.* New York: Farrar, Straus, & Giroux, 2000.

Michael B. Yahuda, *Hong Kong: China's Challenge.* New York: Routledge, 1996.

Boris N. Yeltsin, *The Struggle for Russia.* New York: Times Books, 1994.

Dingxin Zhao, *The Power of Tiananmen: State-Society Relations and the 1989 Beijing Student Movement.* Chicago: University of Chicago Press, 2001.

INDEX

Toffler, Van, 49
totipotency, 160–61

Volberding, Paul, 26

Wang Zhenyao, 90
Washington Post (newspaper), 34
Way of the Torah (newsletter),
  149
al-Wazir, Halil, 82
Weisman, Joel, 33
West Germany, effects of fall of
  communism on, 100, 104, 127
William, Dan, 37, 39, 40
Wilmut, Ian, 155
  on benefits of cloning, 168–70
  on ethics of cloning, 170–71
  on human cloning, 166–67
World Health Organization

(WHO), 61
World Wide Web
  creation of, 118–23
  demonstration of, 123

Ya'akobi, Gad, 80
Ya'ari, Ehud, 73
Yanaev, Gennady, 124
Yaroshinskaya, Alla, 66
Yeltsin, Boris, 19, 125
Yosef, Ovadiah, 148
"You Better Run" (music video),
  48
Yugoslavia
  breakup of, 21–22
  fall of Soviet Union and, 127

Zhao Ziyang, 84, 85
Zhu Rongji, 89